D1329537

MAKING SENSE *of the*
OLD TESTAMENT

RONALD V. EVANS

Ronald V. Evans

 FriesenPress

Suite 300 - 990 Fort St
Victoria, BC, V8V 3K2
Canada

www.friesenpress.com

Copyright © 2018 by Ronald V. Evans
First Edition — 2018

All rights reserved.

Map design by Kathleen and Bill Sowerby.

No part of this book may be used or reproduced by any means, graphic, electronic, or mechanical, including photocopying, recording, taping or by any information storage system without the written permission of the author except in the case of brief quotations embodied in critical articles and reviews.

All scripture quotations are from the ESV® Bible (The Holy Bible, English Standard Version®, published by HarperCollins Publishers, © 2001 by Crossway.
Used by permission. All rights reserved.
The Merneptah Stele: courtesy of the Egyptian Museum, Cairo.
The Cyrus Cylinder: courtesy of the British Museum, London.

ISBN
978-1-5255-2823-1 (Hardcover)
978-1-5255-2824-8 (Paperback)
978-1-5255-2825-5 (eBook)

1. RELIGION, BIBLICAL CRITICISM & INTERPRETATION

Distributed to the trade by The Ingram Book Company

MAKING SENSE *of the*
OLD TESTAMENT

CONTENTS

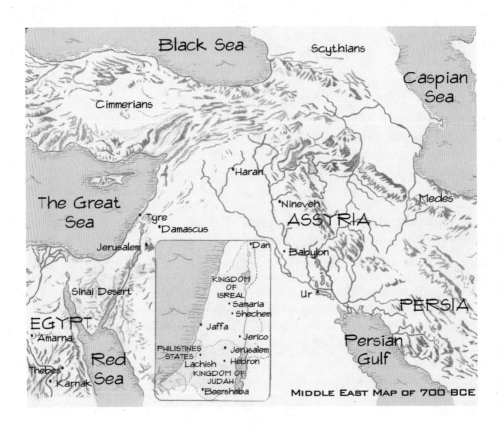

Old Testament Map (c. 700 BCE)

Contents

ACKNOWLEDGEMENTS

I wish to thank my wife Lois and my friend Ian Dale for their support and encouragement in writing this book.

To those who have read and edited my manuscripts, I offer my sincere thanks. Thank you also for your suggestions and insights.

+ Ian Dale
+ Rhonda Milligan
+ Randi Evans
+ William Evans

I also owe a debt of gratitude to John Nelson and Allen Irwin (AVM Tech Services) for assisting me with their computer and graphics skills.

INTRODUCTION

H AVE YOU READ the Old Testament—all thirty-nine books from Genesis to Malachi? If you have, you know how challenging it is to read these ancient texts. The language is archaic with names and places that are alien to your ears. Some of the stories don't flow smoothly or chronologically. Consequently, in spite of good intentions, people seldom read the Old Testament and when they do, they often feel confused and discouraged.

In 2013 when I wrote *Faith of Our Fathers Under the Microscope of Reason and History*, I included a few stories from Genesis, the first book in the Bible. Some of my readers liked my commentaries and asked me to write a book that would make sense of the rest of the Old Testament. Initially I balked at the idea because I knew it would be a time-consuming task for me and my proof-readers who would be critiquing my work.

Obviously (otherwise you would not be reading this paragraph), I decided that making sense of the Old Testament was a laudable project, provided that I included the historical context. When you read the Old Testament in its historical setting, it is not such a daunting book to understand. For example, in the Book of Jonah the prophet is swallowed by a great fish and after three days and three nights, regurgitated onto dry land. It may seem like a children's fable, but as you will see when you read chapter twelve, the story of Jonah resonates with meaning in its context of Assyrian history.

Before I could begin my summaries and commentaries, I needed to update my background in Near Eastern History (my undergraduate minor) and in the Old Testament, which I had studied in a Masters of Divinity programme at Emmanuel College of the University of Toronto from 1956-59. Consequently, I reviewed books by historians, archaeologists, and biblical scholars whose works had not been written when I graduated. I also utilized the internet—an incredible reservoir of knowledge.

I began writing this book on October 11, 2015. I was eighty, an age when many octogenarians hesitate to buy green bananas. Some of my friends thought I should be on a cruise ship sipping wine. My close friends and family disagreed. They understand my passion for ancient history and biblical studies.

I knew I needed to raise three crucial questions before writing the first chapter—**who** were the authors who compiled the Old Testament, and **when** and **why** did they do so? To answer these questions, we have to go back to 587 BCE, to the reign of Nebuchadnezzar II of Babylon. What happened during his reign was catastrophic for the Jewish people. After he pillaged and destroyed their sacred temple in Jerusalem, he exiled many of their leading citizens to Babylon—as slaves.

He carried away all Jerusalem, and all the officials and all the mighty men of valour, 10,000 captives, and all the craftsmen and the smiths. None remained except the poorest people of the land. (2 Kings 24:14).

While in Babylon, the captive Jews were allowed to keep their Sabbath ordinances, a kosher diet, and the practice of circumcision. Many of these exiled Hebrews resisted being assimilated and refused to intermarry with their overseers. Remarkably, they succeeded. They kept their faith and traditions intact through decades of exile. In 539 BCE, thanks to the military successes of the Persians and a decree by Cyrus the Great, the Jewish slaves were freed and 42,360 returned to their homeland. (See the Book of Ezra, chapter 2.)

Some of the returnees were shocked and angered because those who had not been exiled had been negligent in following their Jewish laws—particularly the one that prohibited inter-marriage with non-Jews. It is an understatement to say that there was a serious loss of identity both for those returning from captivity and for those who had been left behind.

For both groups, their faith had been sorely tried. They had been taught that God, from the time of Abraham, had promised that the land of Canaan belonged to them and their descendants forever. Yet they had lost control of the Promised Land. Their king, Zedekiah, after being forced to witness the execution of his sons, had been blinded and carted off to Babylon. Their sacred temple in Jerusalem was a pile of rubble. It had been a focal point for worship and sacrifice since its construction by King Solomon. In the aftermath of all these calamities, it is little wonder that they questioned whether or not they were still a nation, the chosen people of God.

The returning priests and scribes addressed this loss of faith and identity. First, they began the task of rebuilding the temple. Second, they decided that the Jewish people needed an official history. They needed scribes to tell their narrative from their earliest beginnings. They needed an epic, sacred book to restore their pride as a nation of God—a book that would give them purpose and hope, a book that would inspire them to follow their Judaic laws and traditions.

Thus the trauma of the Exile became the motivation for the compilation of the Old Testament. As you will see in the following chapters, this is the scholarly conclusion of biblical experts and is crucial to our understanding of the Old Testament.

In the first thirteen chapters, I will focus on the Jewish narrative from Adam and Eve to the Prophet Daniel. In many respects the narrative will read like a morality play. It is an important story that helps us understand what subsequently happened to Jewish communities in the Roman Empire era, the Middle Ages, and the first half of the Twentieth Century—including the United Nations' decision to create the State of Israel in 1948. So, I cordially invite you to read and critique my summaries and commentaries, and as history students often do, to look at the past as a bridge to our understanding of the present.

✍ Author's Notes

+ All scriptural quotations are from The ESV® Bible. HarperCollins *Publishers,* © 2001 *by Crossway.*
+ I use "Hebrews" and "Jews" interchangeably.
+ I frequently use the abbreviation O.T. for "Old Testament".
+ I often refer to God as "the Lord" or "Yahweh" (as does the Old Testament).
+ I use BCE (Before the Common Era) rather than BC (Before Christ). It's politically correct.
+ I use CE (Common Era) rather than AD (Anno Domini: year of our Lord).
+ The language of the O.T. is not gender neutral. With my apologies, I use the masculine language of the Bible.
+ Just before this introduction you will find a map that will help orientate you to the geography of the O.T.
+ When I refer to "Israel", I mean the northern area of Canaan with Samaria as the capital.
+ When I refer to "Judah", I mean the southern area of Canaan with Jerusalem as the capital.
+ The "Addenda" are supplementary sources of information. Some are actually interesting.

CHAPTER 1

"In the Beginning..."

PICTURE IN YOUR mind one of the Hebrew scribes who returned to Jerusalem from the city of Babylon after Cyrus II of Persia had freed all the slaves in the Persian Empire. During his captivity he had been assigned to work in the city's main library, renowned for its collection of ancient documents including clay tablets from an earlier Sumerian civilization. With this background and his fluency in several Semitic languages, he was chosen to join other scholars in compiling the history of Israel. It was a challenging task because there were many texts, old and new, from which to choose and then edit. There was also an oral tradition of stories and events handed down from previous generations.

These compilers decided that the history of Israel should begin with God when he created the earth and the heavens. They had two Hebrew documents from which to choose: Genesis 1:1-27 and Genesis 2:4-24. In the first document, God (with the Hebrew name of Elohim) created everything in six days. On the sixth day Elohim created man "in our image" and then rested on the seventh day, the Sabbath. In the second document, God (named Yahweh Elohim) first created the Earth and the Heavens. Next He created Adam and then the trees and plants. Lastly, after all the animals had been created, God created Eve as a companion for Adam. Adam was in charge; he was to have dominion over the earth.

Commentary

Even though these are two separate, independent documents, the scribes included both stories. They were oblivious to the scientific discrepancies that we can see in these creation stories. For example, in the first account Elohim created light on the first day so that there would be day and night, but it was not until the fourth day that He created the sun. Another problem is that Elohim created plant life before the sun, but plants require the energy of the sun for photosynthesis to occur. The second creation story is even more problematic because God created man first, then the Garden of Eden with plants and trees, then the rivers, next the animals and birds, and lastly woman!

To be fair, the authors of these two ancient stories were not scientists with backgrounds in biology, geography, astronomy or geology. They thought the earth was flat, a firmament that floated on water, and above that there was another firmament with luminous lights. The message, however, is clear. Both accounts of creation have the same central theological message—"In the beginning God ..."

In addition to these two Hebrew documents, our scribes would have known creation stories from other sources. The earliest yet discovered comes from a Sumerian clay tablet excavated at Nippur (dated c.1600 BCE) and named the Eridu Genesis by historian Thorkild Jacobsen. This tablet refers to the creation of the world and mankind, and a great flood. Another source that preceded the Hebrew stories is the Babylonian/Sumerian story of creation by the gods "Enki" and "Ninti". In this story Ninti created man from clay and by the power of words (incantations). If you use the internet, you can find these two creation stories and see the interesting parallels to the Genesis texts.

According to the scribes of Genesis, God created the cosmos (Earth and all the stars in the heavens) in six days

"In the Beginning..."

approximately 4,000 years ago (based on the genealogies listed in Genesis). Many people in North America accept this timeline as fact. According to a June 2, 2014 Gallup poll, 42% of those surveyed believed in the Creationist view of human origins—an "instant" creation in six days c. 6,000 years ago (4,000 plus 2000 years of the Christian Era). This is astonishing when you consider the geological evidence that dates the Earth as 4.55 billion years old.

Consequently, in Addendum A I have summarized two geological clocks that are used to estimate the age of our planet. The first "clock" is that of fossils and sedimentary rocks, and the second is that of radioactive decay. This addendum also explains carbon dating.

ADAM AND EVE—THE FIRST MAN AND THE FIRST WOMAN

From the creation of the cosmos our scribes moved to the next topic in Israel's narrative—Adam and Eve (the First Man and the First Woman). This story raises important questions about life. Why is survival such a struggle requiring arduous labour for shelter and food? Why do we have pain, suffering and death? The story of Adam and Eve addresses these universal questions.

In Genesis, chapters 2 to 4, God made Adam "in his own image" and gave him a Garden of Eden in which to live. Although Adam had the company of many animals, Adam was lonely and so, from one of Adam's ribs, God created Eve, the first woman. God gave them only one rule— they were not to eat the fruit of the tree of knowledge of good and evil. A talking serpent persuaded Eve to eat this forbidden fruit and she in turn persuaded Adam to taste the fruit. Immediately, they realized they were naked and hid when they heard the footsteps of God walking in the garden. God, angry that they had broken his commandment, cursed and punished them. He decreed that Eve would suffer great pain in childbirth and be ruled by her husband, Adam, who would have to toil and sweat to survive. Then God announced the final punishment—they would no longer be immortal for they and their children, and their children's children, would all die. Then they were driven from the Garden of Eden.

✍ Author's Note

I apologize for digressing but I thought you might enjoy an anatomical tidbit. Many have theorized that the forbidden fruit was the humble apple. Apparently, when Adam took a bite of the apple it stuck in his throat and thus we have the term "Adam's apple" for our laryngeal protrusion.

Commentary

My first observation is that the God of Eden is anthropomorphic—He walks and talks as we do. He has a human form, the inspiration for many medieval paintings in which God is portrayed as a man with a flowing white beard. God has human reactions including anger and vengeance. God is not always fair, for in punishing Adam and Eve he also punishes their children and all future generations. Nor is God all-knowing. He doesn't realize that Adam and Eve had eaten the forbidden fruit until he sees them hiding in the garden. As an aside, how could Adam and Eve know that they were doing anything wrong by eating the forbidden fruit if they had no concept of good and evil?

This story is similar to other earlier creation stories of Mesopotamian cultures. In the Sumerian epic "Enki and Ninhursag: A Paradise Myth", we find a description of Dilman, an idyllic land where animals live peacefully with each other and where humans never experience sickness, aging, or death. There is also an interesting reference to Enki's sore rib. It is reasonable to assume that as the Hebrews settled in Canaan, they would have heard these stories and incorporated them into their own stories of Adam and Eve, and the Garden of Eden.

A surprising number of people in North America take the story of Adam and Eve literally. This is an unfortunate interpretation because it ignores the scientific evidence and portrays God as a heartless, fickle, unforgiving, vengeful deity. It also turns poor Eve into a scapegoat for the woes of humanity, a scapegoat to be blamed and dominated by men for future eons.

On the other hand, if we read the story of Adam and Eve as folklore, we can empathize with the early Hebrews as they struggled to make sense of their existence and hardships. Why did they have to labour so intensely to survive? Why did they and their children have to suffer and die? The answer in the story of Adam and Eve is that the first Man and Woman disobeyed God and, consequently, were responsible for the dire consequences that followed.

For readers who believe in the story of Adam and Eve as history and not as folklore, I have included Addendum B (molecular genetics). According to our DNA, Homo sapiens (modern man) migrated from Africa about 60,000 years ago. It is a remarkable discovery that completely undermines the racist teachings of white supremacists.

CHAPTER 2

The Great Flood
(Noah and the Ark)

~~~~~~~~~~~~~~~~

SUMMARY OF GENESIS: CHAPTERS 5-8

OUR SCRIBES, AFTER pondering about what to write next, decided to include an ancient story that must have been recounted for many generations—the story of Noah and his family surviving a devastating flood. First, however, they wanted to establish an historical link between the first man, Adam, and Noah so that there would be continuity in their narrative. Thus in Genesis 5:1-32, they listed the male genealogy from Adam to Noah. It consists of only ten generations! This is a very small number but mathematically possible because, according to the scribes, many of the ancestors had long lives. Adam lived 930 years and Methuselah died when he was 969 years old.

Ten generations after Adam, Noah was born. Noah was a righteous man, the only man blameless in his generation. The Lord saw that the wickedness of man was great in the earth. Regretting that he had made man, the Lord said, "I will blot out man whom I have created from the face of the land, man and animals and creeping things and birds of the heavens, for I am sorry that I have made them".

God, however, decided to save eight people—Noah, his wife, their three sons and three daughters-in-law. God commanded Noah to build an ark. "And of every living thing of all flesh, you shall bring two of every sort into the ark to keep them alive with you. They shall be male and female". Noah obeyed. He built the ark and brought in two of every species.

Then it rained for forty days and nights. "And the waters prevailed so mightily on the earth that all the high mountains under the whole heaven were covered...and all flesh died that moved on the earth...and the waters prevailed on the earth for 150 days". When the water finally receded, the ark came to rest on a mountain. More time passed until finally the earth was dry and Noah set free his family and all the creatures. Then Noah built an altar and offered burnt offerings. "And when the Lord smelt the pleasing aroma, the Lord said in his heart, 'I will never again curse the ground because of man...neither will I ever again strike down every living creature as I have done'".

Commentary

The scribes who compiled the chronology in Genesis chapter five did so in the sixth century BCE and would have relied on folklore and oral traditions passed on by many previous generations. Outside of the Bible we have no external evidence to validate either their chronology or genealogy.

According to Gallup polls conducted in the last three decades, a significant number of North Americans teach their children that the story of Noah and the Ark is true. In a 2011 Gallup poll three out of ten Americans interpreted the Bible literally as the actual word of God. Consequently I have written Addendum C so that you can consider whether or not this story is folklore or factual.

There is considerable evidence that there was a great flood between the Tigris and Euphrates Rivers. In 1922 Leonard Woolley, a British archaeologist, made an important discovery during excavations at the ancient Canaanite city of Ur. He unearthed an eight-foot layer of clay and silt that matched the sediments of the nearby river Euphrates. Geologically he dated this layer to c. 2800 BCE. His discovery supported the oral stories of a flood disaster—not a global one for which there is no archaeological or geological evidence, but a local, devastating flood.

There is also reason to believe that our scribes borrowed extensively from a much earlier flood story discovered in 1853 at Nineveh called *The Epic of Gilgamesh* (Tablet XI, written on clay tablets and carbon dated to c. 2500 BCE). In this story, Enlil, the chief divinity of the Sumerian gods, was so angry with mankind that he persuaded the gods to destroy humanity by a great flood. But the god Ea or Enki took pity on a virtuous man called Uta-Napishtim. He was told to build a huge boat so that he could save himself, his kin, and all the living things that he could load onto the six decks of his boat. Uta did as he was told. The walls were each ten times twelve cubits (a cubit was c. 20") in height. With six decks, the boat was huge, like a field. "All the living beings that I had I loaded on it, I had all my kith and kin go up to the boat, all the beasts". When the storm finally subsided after six days and seven nights, the boat was safely lodged on a mountain.

"When a seventh day arrived I sent forth a dove and released it. The dove went off, but came back to me; I sent forth a swallow and released it. The swallow went off, but came back to me. I sent forth a raven and released it. The raven went off, and saw the waters slither back. It eats, it scratches, it bobs, but does not circle back to me. Then I sent out everything in all directions and sacrificed. I offered incense in front of the mountain-ziggurat. Seven and seven cult vessels I put in place . . . . the gods smelled the sweet savor, and collected like flies over a (sheep) sacrifice".

The similarities to Genesis are many. The God of Genesis is disturbingly similar to the unpredictable Sumerian gods who talk and walk and display human emotions. In the Epic of Gilgamesh, humans had good reason to be fearful of these powerful and capricious gods. The gods were responsible for every catastrophe. Therefore humans had to be both respect-ful and wary of the gods—placating them with sacrifices, pleasing odours, and rituals. The flood hero, Uta-Napishtim, is a heroic symbol of man surviving the wrath of the gods.

The two stories are also similar in theology. In both stories God gives up on the human race, except for one family. He is so angry and vengeful that he kills all but one family. He drowns innocent children, innocent animals, innocent birds and insects, and all the trees and flowers.

> All things bright and beautiful,
> All creatures great and small,
> All things wise and wonderful,
> The Lord God drowned them all.

Christian apologists (from a Greek word meaning defend-ers) often dismiss The Epic of Gilgamesh contending that the Sumerians copied and modified their story from that of the Bible. The apologists who use this argument forget that from c.1900 to 1300 BCE the Hebrews were nomads who followed their herds and lived in tents. Nomadic tribes were not likely to have educated scribes with the requisite materials of clay tablets, kilns and papyrus on which to record stories or events. On the other hand, during this period extensive records have been found in **urban** settlements such as Ur, Nineveh, Ugarit, Babylon, Alexandria, Luxor and Nippur.

Although our scribes had more stories to include in the Book of Genesis such as those of Cain and Abel, and the Tower of Babel, I am going to move forward to the next important period recorded by our scribes—that of the Patriarchs.

✍ Author's Note

In Genesis from chapters 11-16, the first patriarch is named Abram, meaning "high father". After God made a sacred covenant with Abram (chapter 17), God changed his name to Abraham meaning "father of a multitude".

CHAPTER 3

The Patriarchs

~~~~~~~~~~~~

THE PATRIARCHS OF the O.T. are revered as "men of God". Their names and deeds are recorded in the first book of the Bible, Genesis, chapters 11-44. When you read these chapters, you find some fascinating anecdotes—substitute "wives", talking angels, famines and plagues, a sixty-five year old wife of irresistible beauty, a boy bound on an altar about to be sacrificed by his father, disinherited sons, rape and revenge, murder, incest, and a mother breast-feeding her child at the age of ninety.

ABRAHAM (GENESIS—CHAPTERS 11 TO 17)

His story began when his father, Terah, moved his family from the city of Ur (near the mouth of the Euphrates River in today's Iraq) to the Assyrian city of Haran. While in Haran, Abraham married his half-sister Sarah. Unable to conceive, Sarah ordered Hagar, her slave, to sleep with her husband. Abraham voiced no objections, and in time Hagar became pregnant. Sarah must have had second thoughts about the "handmaiden". Whatever her reasons, she treated Hagar so harshly she fled into the wilderness. There, an angel of the Lord rescued her, and Hagar obeyed the angel's instructions to return and to submit to her mistress. Her baby was born and was called Ishmael, the first-born male child of Abraham.

While in Haran before journeying to Canaan, Abraham had a revelation from God—*I will make of you a great nation, and I will bless you, and make your name great . . . and in you all the families of the earth shall be blessed".* When Abraham arrived in the land of Canaan, *Then the Lord appeared to Abram and said, To your offspring I will give this land.* In Genesis 15:18 this promise is described as a covenant between God and Abram. *To your offspring I give this land, from the river of Egypt to the great river, the river Euphrates.* This promise is repeated even more strongly in Genesis 17:8. *And I will give to you and to your offspring after you the land of your sojourning, all the land of Canaan, for an everlasting possession, and I will be their God.*

Commentary

This revelation and covenant are quoted throughout the O.T. as proof that Canaan belonged to the Israelites as a divine right. That was the viewpoint of the scribes and priests who compiled the O.T. in the sixth century BCE and who claimed to know what God had promised to Abraham c. 1900 BCE.

 This tenet of faith has been contentiously debated for centuries by Jews, Palestinians, Christians, and Muslims. For those who accept the O.T. as the inerrant Word of God, there is no debate.

Before Abraham reached the promised land of Canaan, he journeyed to Egypt because of a great famine. When the Pharaoh learned of the great beauty of Sarah (sixty-five years old), he desired her and sent for her. As instructed by her husband, Sarah pretended to be his sister, not his wife. God, displeased at this deception, sent plagues upon the Pharaoh and his household. When the Pharaoh learned that Sarah was married, he sent her back to Abraham and ordered them to leave Egypt. This story is told in Genesis, chapter 12. Later, in chapter 20, Abraham repeated the deception with Abimelech, King of Gerar, who also had heard of the beautiful "sister" of Abraham, and had sent for her. Before the king could consummate the relationship, he had a disturbing dream in which God threatened him with death for taking another man's wife. Abimelech hastily returned Sarah along with gifts of sheep and oxen, and male and female slaves.

When Abraham was ninety, God promised that he would be the father of a multitude of nations (Genesis 17: 4), but ten years later Sarah still had not given birth to a child. She despaired that she would ever provide Abraham with an heir and with good reason because *The way of women had ceased to be with Sarah.* This was a discreet reference to menopause. God, though, kept his promise. Sarah conceived and at the age of ninety (Abraham was one hundred) bore a son named Isaac, whom she nursed!

In Genesis 22, God used the child Isaac to test Abraham. "*Take your son, your only son Isaac, whom you love, and go to the land of Moriah, and offer him there as a burnt offering on one of the mountains of which I shall tell you.* Abraham intended to obey God, but just before he sacrificed Isaac an angel of the Lord intervened, praised Abraham for fearing God, and provided Abraham with a ram caught by his horns in a nearby thicket . . . *and Abraham went and took the ram and offered it up as a burnt offering instead of his son.*

Commentary

Twice, Abraham pretended his wife was his sister knowing full well what would happen to her after the Pharaoh and Abimelech "sent" for her. What kind of a husband would treat his wife like a sexual commodity? What kind of justice was dispensed by God? God neither reprimanded nor punished Abraham; instead he was rewarded!

The story of Abraham obeying God's command to sacrifice his first-born son Isaac was taught to me in Sunday school as an inspiring example of faith and obedience. Now, many decades later, I find the story disturbing. Even though I now interpret the story metaphorically, I still can't help imagining the feelings and thoughts of a boy, bound and laying on a pile of wood on an altar, watching his father approach him with a knife in his hand. What kind of God would set such a cruel test? What kind of father would comply?

In the story of Abraham, we see the importance of sacrifice to the Hebrew people. Throughout the O.T. we find many instances and descriptions of Levite priests offering animal sacrifices to God. According to biblical scribes, the Creator of the universe, the One who created all the plants and animals on Earth was pleased and honoured by the slaughter and burning of animals (preferably unblemished). This was the perspective of the patriarchs, according to the scribes who pieced together the narrative of Abraham.

After Sarah died, Abraham married Keturah who gave him six sons. Shortly before Abraham died, at the age of 175, we are told that "Abraham gave all that he had to Isaac". There is no mention of Abraham giving any inheritance to his first-born son, Ishmael, perhaps because his mother, Hagar, was a slave. Nor does he leave anything to his six sons from his second wife, Keturah. Nor does Abraham leave anything for his nameless and unmentioned daughters, but to the sons of his concubines, he gave gifts (Genesis 25:1-6).

My granddaughter has a tee-shirt that says, "Boys Drool and Girls Rule". In this era the Patriarchs ruled. Abraham is revered in the Bible (and the Koran) as a man of God, a mighty prophet of old. If the stories of Abraham are true, then I have a much different picture of him, and it is not at all complimentary. But are the stories of Abraham based on history or folklore?

A few years ago I attended a lecture by a guest rabbi on the Old Testament at McMaster University in Hamilton, Ontario. After the lecture I asked him if he thought Abraham was an historical person. I have never forgotten his answer: "Abraham is an interpretation of an interpretation."

We also tend to think of the patriarchs Isaac and Jacob as spiritual mentors, men of character and great faith. Were they? I wonder what you will think after you read the following summaries and stories.

THE PATRIARCHS ISAAC AND JACOB
(GENESIS CHAPTERS 24-50)

+ Abraham's son Isaac took Rebekah as his wife and their first-born were twins: Esau and Jacob. Esau was born first.

+ Due to a famine, Isaac moved with his family and herds to Gerar, home to Abimelech the Philistine king. As his father did forty years ago, he introduced the beautiful Rebekah as his sister because he was afraid the Philistines might kill him in order to take Rebekah. Abimelech learned of this deception and ordered his men to leave Isaac and Rebekah alone.

+ When Isaac was old "and his eyes were dim", Jacob pretended to be Esau in order to receive a sacred blessing to succeed his father; in other words, Jacob swindled Esau, the first-born son, out of his rightful inheritance.

+ Jacob worked for seven years for his uncle, Alban, in order to marry his first-love, Rachel. After the marriage to his veiled bride, and after their first night together, he discovered in the light of morning that he had married the sister of Rachel, Leah, the first-born daughter. *Perhaps he had way too much wine or he had lost his sense of hearing and touch.* Jacob laboured for seven more years and then married Rachel as his second wife.

+ Jacob had thirteen children—six sons and a daughter (Dinah) by Leah, two sons by Balham (Rachel's maid), two sons by Zillah (Leah's maid), and two sons (Joseph and Benjamin) by Rachel.

+ Jacob's daughter, Dinah, was raped by Shechem. Following the guidelines of Exodus 22:16-17, the young man offered to marry her; his father, Humor, consulted with Jacob and they came to an amicable agreement for marriage. Dinah's brothers, Simeon and Levi, however, were set on revenge and killed all the males of Shechem (the city) including Humor. Jacob's other sons stole all the herds and property they could lay their hands on, including women and children.

+ Jacob favoured Joseph over his other sons. His brothers despised Joseph for this favouritism and for his grandiose dreams in which his brothers bowed down to him. They got their revenge by selling Joseph to a caravan of Ishmaelites on their way to Egypt. Jacob was heart-broken when told that his beloved son had been torn to pieces by a wild beast.

+ In time Joseph became a powerful overseer of the Pharaoh and, predicting a dire famine, stored a bountiful supply of grain in Egypt for the lean years to come. When the famine reached Canaan, Jacob sent his sons to Egypt to trade for grain. Eventually (it is a long story), Joseph was joyously reunited with Jacob and his family. Joseph allowed his brothers, families and herds to live in Egypt.

Commentary

In this patriarchal age, maids were expected to do more than cooking and cleaning. It seems unlikely that Jacob had only one daughter. I suspect that most daughters were not considered important enough to be listed.

It is surprising that Jacob did not reprimand his sons for their treachery, violence and greed. Nor was Jacob criticized for creating an atmosphere of hatred and jealousy by blatant favouritism of Joseph.

According to the scribes who gave us these stories, God was silent—no judgment, no punishment.

I am going to digress from the narrative of the Patriarchs, because I think you will find it interesting to examine the following, bizarre stories of Abraham's nephew, Lot. As you will see, the scribes had their reasons for including the following stories.

THE DESTRUCTION OF SODOM AND GOMORRAH (GENESIS 19)
(Lot's wife is turned into a pillar of salt)

As Abraham sat at the door of his tent, three men approached him, one of whom was either the Lord or a representative of the Lord. The other two are angels. The Lord told Abraham that he had decided to destroy the cities of Sodom and Gomorrah because of their great wickedness. The Patriarch pleaded repeatedly for the lives of the innocent; so the Lord promised that if there were ten righteous individuals in the cities, he would spare the cities from punishment.

The story then shifts to Sodom where Lot was approached by the same two angels. A gracious host, Lot invited the angels to his tent where he washed their feet and prepared a feast for them. Before they retired for the night, the men of Sodom surrounded the house . . . *and they called to Lot, 'Where are the men who came to you tonight? Bring them out to us, that we may know them.'* (In this context the word "know" is a euphemism for sex.)

Lot begged for their safety—*Behold, I have two daughters who have not known any man. Let me bring them out to you, and do to them as you please. Only do nothing to these men.* The crowd was not interested in the virgin daughters (which is a subtle clue to their sexual orientation). When they threatened to break down Lot's door, the angels struck the intruders with blindness.

The next morning, warned of the impending doom, Lot, his wife, and two daughters fled the city. They were instructed not to look back lest they be "consumed". *Then the Lord rained on Sodom and Gomorrah sulphur and fire . . . Lot's wife looked behind her, and she became a pillar of salt . . . and behold, the smoke of the land went up like the smoke of a furnace.*

Lot took refuge in a cave in the hills for months. The daughters, worried that they would never have children, plied their father with wine and took turns lying with him in his drunkenness. Both conceived and had sons—one named Moab who became the forefather of the Moabites and one named Ben-ammi, the forefather of the Ammonites.

Commentary

Some historians have speculated that the story of Sodom and Gomorrah was based on volcanic action. Although there is no geological evidence of volcanic eruptions in Canaan in this era, it is likely that there were stories of similar disasters in the Mediterranean—stories passed on to future generations. For example, we know that in 1628 BCE there was an enormous volcanic eruption that nearly destroyed the island of Santorini in the Aegean Sea. Or the basis for the story of brimstone and fire falling on Sodom and Gomorrah may have been an earthquake with deep fissures that spewed out molten lava.

When such events occurred, ancient seers and priests had a common explanation—someone had displeased the gods. In this story the explanation is similar. The people of Sodom and Gomorrah had sinned and, consequently, God destroyed them. (This story is eerily similar to that of Noah and the Ark when God drowned mankind, except for one family.) Lot's wife, whose home and belongings were burning, could not resist the urge to look back to see what was happening to her home and her neighbours. God showed no empathy and turned her into a pillar of salt.

The incestuous story of Lot and his daughters is as incredible as God turning Lot's wife into a pillar of salt. The daughters plied their father with so much wine that he had

The Patriarchs

no recollection of what he did. It would seem they did this multiple times because both daughters became pregnant. It is an unbelievable story. For most men inebriation is not an aphrodisiac.

Some scholars have speculated that the story of Sodom and Gomorrah was intended as a warning against homosexuality, a great "abomination" (Leviticus 18:22). Maybe the scribes had that in mind. What is morally shocking and puzzling is that God neither reprimanded nor punished Lot and his daughters for their incestuous behaviour.

To the scribes, however, it was important to point out that Lot, a nephew of Abraham, fathered the two boys because Moab became the forefather of the Moabites and Ben-ammi, the forefather of the Ammonites. Later, these two tribes became enemies of the Jews. Thus the inclusion of a story about a drunken Lot sleeping with his daughters could be a not-too-subtle slur directed at the Moabites and the Ammonites.

✍ Author's Note

There were pillars of salt along the coast of the Dead Sea and, in all likelihood, the pillars inspired folklore.

A Concluding Commentary

Outside of the Book of Genesis we know little about the Patriarchs. We have no scrolls, clay tablets, stone monuments, or burial tombs that give us information of the Patriarchs. William G. Dever, an American archaeologist, who specialized in the history of Israel and the Near East in biblical times, came to the following conclusion: "After a century of exhaustive investigation, all respectable archaeologists have given up hope of recovering any context that would make Abraham, Isaac or Jacob credible 'historical figures'" (page 29 of "Who Wrote the Bible"). His comment should come as no surprise when you remember that the scribes who "recorded" the stories of the Patriarchs did so in the sixth century BCE—many centuries after the Patriarch Abraham left Ur.

Before moving on to the next chapter, the Jewish Exodus from Egypt under the leadership of Moses, I need to address the time gap that exists between the patriarchs (c.1900-1700 BCE) and the time of Moses (c.1300 BCE). What happened to the family of Jacob and their ancestors once they reached Egypt? According to Genesis 15:13, they became servants. "Your offspring will be sojourners in a land that is not theirs and will be servants there, and they will be afflicted for four hundred years". How long were they servants? According to Exodus 12:40, "The time that the people of Israel dwelt in Egypt was 430 years".

CHAPTER 4

The Exodus

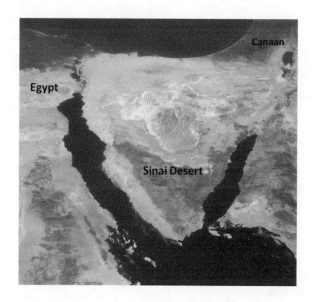

A SUMMARY OF EXODUS CHAPTERS 1 TO 20

THE STORY OF Moses leading the Israelites from Egypt to freedom is an amazing story that has been the inspiration for eleven movies. Drama abounds. The descendants of Joseph, who had previously fled to Egypt in a time of famine, had become slaves. In time they became so numerous that Pharaoh decided to have all newborn Hebrew boys cast into the Nile. One distraught mother set her baby adrift in a bulrush basket hoping someone would save him. The Pharaoh's daughter heard the baby crying, rescued him, named him Moses and raised him as her child.

As a young adult, Moses killed an Egyptian overseer for beating a Hebrew slave and fled into Midian (in the northwest of the Arabian Peninsula). While tending sheep there, Moses heard the voice of God from a bush that burned but was not consumed. God ordered Moses to return to Egypt and to lead the sons of Israel into Canaan, the land He had promised to Abraham and his descendants.

Returning to Egypt Moses became an advocate for the Hebrew slaves, pleading for the freedom of his people, but Pharaoh did not listen. After the Lord punished Egypt with eight successive plagues, Pharaoh reluctantly gave Moses permission to lead his people out of Egypt, but then he changed his mind and pursued them with his army. When Moses reached the Red Sea, he stretched out his arm and parted the waters, so that his people could walk on dry land through the sea. When the Egyptians followed, the Lord ordered Moses to again stretch out his arm over the sea, and the waters returned. Pharaoh, his army, horses and charioteers perished beneath the waves. None survived.

For the next forty years Moses led 600,000 Israeli men, along with their families and animals, through the Sinai desert. When they reached Mount Sinai, Moses has a pivotal meeting with God, and came down from the mountain with two tablets of stone containing the Ten Commandments.

Commentary

According to the inscription at the beginning of the Book of Exodus, the author is Moses. That is also the claim made for Genesis, Leviticus, Deuteronomy and Numbers. There are many reasons why the majority of biblical scholars discount Moses as the author. The most obvious reason is that much of the first five books of the Bible are written in the third person.

Also, authors do not record their own deaths and burials (See Deuteronomy 34:5-6).

Dr. Richard E. Friedman, Professor of Jewish Studies at the University of Georgia, had this to say about the authorship of the first five books of the Bible. "At present there is hardly a biblical scholar in the world actively working on the problem who would claim that the Five Books of Moses were written by Moses—or by any one person" ("Who Wrote the Bible" pg. 28).

I was shocked to learn in my first year of Near Eastern History that the story of the infant Moses set adrift on the Nile River closely resembled the legend of the Sumerian king, Sargon the Great of Akkad (c. 2334-2279 BCE). This legend was discovered in 1867 in the library of Ashurbanipal in Nineveh by the British archaeologist Sir Henry Rawlinson. According to the cuneiform inscription on the engraved stele, Sargon was an orphan set adrift on the Euphrates River by his mother in a reed basket sealed with tar. He was found and raised by a gardener of a Sumerian king. In time Sargon became a trusted advisor to the king. The parallels here to the story of Moses are obvious.

Biblical scholars have had great difficulty in identifying the Pharaoh associated with Moses. Was he Thutmose III, Tutankhamen, Rameses I, Seti I, or Rameses II? Some scholars theorized that it was Rameses II who lived from 1303-1213 BCE; however, if he were the Pharaoh, he would have died at the age of ninety pursuing the eighty-year-old Moses through the desert and the Red Sea! The fact that the scribes did not name the Pharaoh of the Exodus is understandable when you remember that they wrote the story in the sixth century BCE and the Exodus supposedly occurred c. 1300 BCE. The nameless Pharaoh is another clue that the story of the Exodus is based on folklore.

The Pharaoh kept vacillating, promising to let the Israelites go and then changing his mind. In Exodus 9:12, 10:20, 10:27, 11:10 and 14:4 we are given an explanation—"the Lord hardened Pharaoh's heart". If God wanted to exercise his power over the Pharaoh, why did he not "soften" Pharaoh's heart? In sending plague after plague, why did God allow so many innocent people and animals to suffer because of the Pharaoh's decisions? These two questions are only troubling if you interpret the story literally and not as folklore.

FORTY YEARS IN THE SINAI DESERT

For forty years Moses led his people throughout the Sinai desert. According to Exodus 12:37, it was a large number, about 600,000 men plus their families and animals. They survived because God provided water and manna from heaven. On a mountain top (perhaps Mt. Sinai), God appeared to Moses. The mountain trembled, and there was thunder and lightning, fire and smoke, and heralding trumpets. After forty days and nights, Moses came down with stone tablets inscribed with laws written "with the finger" of God.

During these forty days, the people of Israel had been allowed by Aaron to worship a golden calf. When Moses came down from the mountain and saw this idolatry, he was furious and ordered the execution of three thousand men. Then the Lord sent a plague upon the people because they had helped Aaron make the golden calf. After these punishments, Moses reiterated God's promise that they would enter and possess the land of Canaan, a land "flowing with milk and honey".

Commentary

When Moses came down from the mountain after forty days, he was shocked and angered to see his countrymen worshipping a golden calf. Even though Aaron and the rest of the

Hebrews had not yet seen or heard the laws about idolatry given to Moses by God, Moses had three thousand men put to death for their idolatry. This punishment seems draconian. If the scribes who included this story meant it to be understood metaphorically, then the tale becomes a stern and harsh warning about idolatry.

Is the story of the Exodus history or folklore? Consider these five points. One, Moses left Egypt with 603,550 men, but there would have been women and children as well. So it is reasonable to estimate that Moses led 2.5 million Hebrews out of Egypt along with their herds and possessions. The logistics of organizing and leading such a vast number in an arid area without roads is incredible. Imagine the daily challenge of providing sustenance for 2.5 million people and their herds in such an inhospitable place as the Sinai desert.

Two, there are problems with timelines. When Moses began his forty-year trek through the Sinai desert, he was eighty years old, and one hundred and twenty years old when he died. In that era a man was lucky to reach the age of sixty. Moses outlived his contemporaries. All of the men who left Egypt died in the wilderness of Sinai except Moses, Caleb and Joshua! (See Numbers 26:64-66.) There would have been young men eighteen to twenty (much younger than Moses) who fled from Egypt with Moses; yet according to the narrative they all died during the forty-year trek.

Three, while there are many references to Moses and the Exodus in the Pentateuch and the Book of Joshua, there are few references to Moses in the remaining books of the O.T., and where the name "Moses" occurs, it is usually in the context of his laws, not the Exodus. The prophets Amos and Hosea make no mention of Moses or the Exodus. In Jeremiah there is only one reference to Moses and in Isaiah there are only two references. It's astonishing that these important prophets had nothing or little to say about the one who led the people of Israel out of Egypt and gave them God's laws and commandments. This silence is another indication that the story of Moses and the Exodus was written after the lives of Amos and Hosea.

Four, there is no external evidence to corroborate the story of the Exodus. There are no Egyptian records of 2.5 million Hebrew slaves in Egypt, the successive plagues, and the exodus of these slaves led by a leader called Moses. Archaeologists have scoured all the seas in the Sinai region but have yet to find the remains of the army, weapons, chariots and horses of Pharaoh. Nor can archaeologists find any evidence in the Sinai desert of the 2.5 million Hebrews who wandered for forty years in this arid area. After the Hebrews crossed the river Jordan into Canaan, the scribes reported that Joshua and his warriors slaughtered all seven indigenous tribes. Archaeologists, however, have found no physical evidence of this genocide.

Lastly, if the Hebrews had lived in Egypt for four hundred years, you might expect that once they reached Canaan their pottery would have reflected Egyptian designs and techniques, but that is not the case according to anthropologists familiar with Canaanite pottery.

In the last eighteen years a number of Jewish scholars and editors have spoken out about the Exodus including Ze'ev Herzog, Professor of Archaeology at Tel Aviv University. He made the following, shocking statement in a 1999 cover-page article in the Haaretz newspaper: "This is what archaeologists have learned from their excavations in the Land of Israel: The Israelites were never in Egypt, did not wander in the desert, and did not conquer the land in a military campaign."

Dr. Zahi Hawass, an Egyptian archaeologist who served for years as Egypt's Minister of State for Antiquities Affairs, was quite blunt when reporters from the New York Times asked him, in a 2007 interview, if the Exodus were true. Here is his reply: "Really, it's a myth . . . . If they get upset, I don't care. This is my career as an archaeologist. I should tell them the truth. If the people are upset, that is not my problem."

Finkelstein and Mazar are two prominent archaeologists and Israeli professors who concluded, "We cannot perceive a whole nation wandering through the desert for forty years under the leadership of Moses, as presented in the biblical tradition". (See page 60 of "The Quest for the Historical Israel", published in 2007.)

The Jerusalem Post (August 10, 2015) printed the following statement, "The Exodus is so fundamental to us and our Jewish sources that it is an embarrassment that there is no evidence outside of the Bible to support it". This quotation is from a Senior Fellow of the W.F. Albright Institute of Archaeological Research, Jerusalem.

THE DEATH AND BURIAL OF MOSES

Moses died in Moab—a country that bordered Canaan. He was not buried in Canaan, the Promised Land, because he had offended God in the first month of their sojourn in the desert. When the people of Israel arrived at the wilderness of Zin, they asked Moses why he had brought them to this barren wilderness only to die of thirst. Moses and his brother Aaron went into the tabernacle tent and prayed to God. And the Lord said to Moses, "Take the staff, and assemble the congregation . . . and tell the rock before their eyes to yield its water . . ." Moses gathered the people before the rock and said, 'Hear now, you rebels: shall we bring water for you out of this rock?' And Moses lifted up his hand and struck the rock with his staff twice, and water came out abundantly . . ." (Numbers 20:1-12).

What had Moses and Aaron done that was wrong? First, when they pleaded to God for water, they showed a lack of faith. They should have believed God's promise that He would provide for the people of Israel in the wilderness. Second, when Moses struck the rock with the staff, Moses took the credit for the miracle that happened. He said, "We shall bring forth water for you."

The consequences were severe. "And the Lord said to Moses and Aaron, 'Because you did not believe in me, to uphold me as holy in the eyes of the people of Israel, therefore you shall not bring this assembly into the land which I have given them'"(Numbers 20:12). "So Moses the servant of the Lord died there in the land of Moab, according to the word of the Lord, and he buried him in the valley opposite Beth-peor; but no one knows the place of his burial to this day" (Deuteronomy 34:5).

Commentary

The phrase "to this day" suggests the passage of time—a recounting long after his demise. We are told that Joshua led the Hebrews into the Promised Land. It is reasonable to assume that Joshua, the successor of Moses, would have known where they buried their leader. On the other hand, if modern biblical scholars are correct that the story of the Exodus was written in the sixth century BCE, then it is understandable why no one knew the burial site of Moses seven hundred years later.

You have to feel sorry for Moses. After all he had done, organizing the Hebrew slaves in Egypt, saving them from bondage and leading them for forty years in the desert wilderness of Sinai, he is not allowed to enter the Promised Land because God was piqued, hurt and resentful for what happened at Zin. God was unwilling to forgive Moses and Aaron for a few moments of weakness and pride.

✍ Author's Notes

Whenever I read the book of Exodus, I keep reminding myself that this story was written in the sixth century BCE at a crucial time for the Jews in exile and for those who remained in Canaan. The Babylonians under Nebuchadnezzar had ruthlessly killed all the sons of King Zedekiah, blinded the king, and carried him off to Babylon along with many Jewish religious leaders, and to add insult to injury, the Babylonians had pillaged and destroyed the Temple of Jerusalem.

It was in such a context that the scribes included the story of the Exodus in their narrative to inspire and unify their people, and in this regard they succeeded remarkably. Consequently, the Exodus story became the basis for many of the festivals and holy days of the Jewish Year by which Jews celebrated their escape from slavery, their birth as a nation under Moses, and the giving of the Torah to Moses on Mount Sinai. These were important events, celebrated in the synagogues and also in the intimacy of their homes. They were (and still are) celebrations that helped Jews to retain their identity.

I see a parallel here for Christians in the celebration of Christmas. While some conservative Christians believe the nativity stories to be historical truths, other more liberal Christians interpret the Christmas story with its vivid imagery of a guiding star, angelic hosts, shepherds and wise men bearing gifts, as a beautiful allegory. In either case the spiritual focus is the same—to celebrate the birth of Jesus as God's gift of love to the world. Even agnostics and atheists celebrate Christmas, not as a religious event, but as a celebration of family and "goodwill to men".

While I can understand why some Jews are embarrassed to discover that the Exodus is folklore, I think that Jews will continue to celebrate the Exodus as a symbol of the persecution they have endured through the ages, and as a poignant reminder of their determined quest for freedom and independence. The Passover celebrations bring Jewish people together in synagogues and also in private family settings. They are important cultural celebrations.

CHAPTER 5

The Conquest of Canaan

~~~~~~~~~~~~~~~

MOSES, JOSHUA, AARON, JUDAH—HEROIC
LEADERS OR INFAMOUS LEGENDS?

ACCORDING TO THE books of Exodus, Leviticus, Numbers, Deuteronomy, and Joshua, these were the men who led the Hebrews to Canaan, the Promised Land. Under the command of Joshua, the Hebrew warriors obliterated seven tribes: the Hittites, the Girgashites, the Amorites, the Canaanites, the Perizzites, the Hivites, and the Jebusites. You can read the details of this conquest in the Book of Joshua, Chapters 6-12. Some of the stories are incredibly violent.

Consider for example the story of Joshua capturing the city of Jericho. "And the Lord said to Joshua, 'See, I have given into your hand Jericho, with its king and mighty men of valour. You shall march round the city . . . . Thus shall you do for six days. Seven priests shall bear seven trumpets of rams' horns before the ark. On the seventh day you shall march around the city seven times, and the priests shall blow the trumpets. And when they make a long blast with the ram's horn, when you hear the sound of the trumpet, then all the people shall shout with a great shout, and the wall of the city will fall down flat' . . . . As soon as the people heard the sound of the trumpet, the people shouted a great shout, and the wall fell down flat, so that the people went up into the city . . . and they captured the city. Then they devoted all in the city to destruction, both men and women, young and old, oxen, sheep, and donkeys, with the edge of the sword."

In addition to wiping out every man, woman, child and animal in Jericho, the Hebrews, with a force of 12,000 warriors, attacked the Midianites (See Numbers Chapter 31). "They warred against Midian, as the Lord commanded Moses, and killed every male ... and the people of Israel took captive the women of Midian and their little ones ... And Moses was angry with the officers of the army .... Moses said to them, 'Have you let all the women live? Behold, these, on Balaam's advice, caused the people of Israel to act treacherously against the Lord in the incident of Peor, and so the plague came among the congregation of the Lord. Now therefore, kill every male among the little ones, and kill every woman who has known man by lying with him. But all the young girls who have not known man by lying with him, keep alive for yourselves.'" In addition to the 32,000 virgins who were "spared", there were other "spoils of war" to be divided among the conquerors: 675,000 sheep, 72,000 cattle, and 61,000 donkeys.

Commentary

Fortunately, there is no evidence of the genocide that is alleged to have happened under Joshua. As you read the Book of Judges, you discover that the seven indigenous tribes were not wiped out. You also have grounds for questioning what was alleged to have happened at Jericho and Midia. There is no archaeological evidence of the mayhem and violence detailed in the Book of Joshua or the Book of Numbers. Nor do we have any Near Eastern records of these events in the ancient libraries of Ugarit, Babylon or Alexandria.

It is important to keep in mind that the scribes of the sixth century BCE recounted their grandiose stories of Jericho and the Midianites many centuries after the "conquest" of Canaan. I used the adjective "grandiose" in referring to Joshua's claims of victories. Here is a prime example in

Joshua 10: 12-13. "Then spoke Joshua to the Lord in the day when the Lord gave the Amorites over to the men of Israel; and he said in the sight of Israel, 'Sun, stand thou still at Gideon, and thou Moon in the valley of Aijalon.' And the sun stood still, and the moon stayed, until the nation took vengeance on their enemies."

Archaeologist Dame Kathleen Mary Kenyon (Principal of St. Hugh's College, Oxford) conducted extensive excavations at Jericho. She found that in the time-frame of the Exodus (1300-1250 BCE) Jericho lay completely abandoned. She did find evidence of earlier walls in ruin. She surmised that the walls of Jericho could have collapsed due to an earthquake. "It would have been very natural for the Israelites to have regarded such a visitation as divine intervention." (pg 262 "Digging Up Jericho")

Conservative literalists have a two-fold challenge in explaining the conquest of Canaan. The first is the lack of external evidence, and the second is theological; namely, why would a beneficent God sanction and condone the atrocities committed by the Hebrews under the leadership of Moses, Aaron, Joshua, and Judah? This would be the same God who gave Moses the Ten Commandments, one of which prohibits killing.

Most biblical scholars, such as those listed at the end of this chapter, think that the "conquest" was relatively peaceful and took place gradually over several hundreds of years. In "The Bible Unearthed" (2001), Finkelstein and Silberman summarized the archaeological surveys done since 1967 in the traditional territories of the tribes of Judah, Benjamin, Ephraim, and Manasseh. They discovered a network of Israelite villages characterized by their pottery, a lack of pig bones, and the practice of circumcision. They found no evidence of a violent invasion of Canaan. Their portrayal of Israelite communities that emerged peacefully c. 1200 BCE is *also shared by Professor Robert Karl Gnuse PH.D. (1997) in "No Other Gods: Emergent Monotheism in Israel".*

SCHOLARS WHO CONCLUDED THAT THE OCCUPATION OF CANAAN WAS PEACEFUL

Dr. John Van Seters (*Abraham in History and Tradition*)

Dr. William Dever (*Who Were the Early Israelites and Where Did They Come From*)

Dr. Bruce M. Metzger (*The Oxford Companion to the Bible*)

Dr Israel Finkelstein, Israeli archaeologist, (*The Bible Unearthed*)

Dr. Philip Davies (*In Search of Ancient Israel*)

Dr. Kurt L. Noll (*Canaan an Israel in Antiquity: An Introduction*)

Dr. Brad E. Kelle (*Biblical History and Israel's Past*) with co-writer Megan Bishop Moore

Dr. Donald Redford, Egyptologist and Archaeologist, (*Egypt, Canaan and Israel in Ancient Times*)

The Conquest of Canaan

CHAPTER 6

The Ten Commandments

IN THIS CHAPTER you will find the Ten Commandments (as recorded in Exodus 20:3-17), my commentaries, and a brief description of three additional moral codes from the Middle East—those of the Sumerian king Ur-Nammu, the Babylonian king, Hammurabi, and an Egyptian Theban scribe. As you read this chapter, I suggest you consider these two questions. How inclusive are the Ten Commandments as a moral compass, and how original are the Ten Commandments?

COMMANDMENTS # 1-3

"You shall have no other gods before me. You shall not make for yourself a carved image, or any likeness of anything that is in heaven above, or that is in the earth beneath, or that is in the water under the earth. You shall not bow down to them or serve them, for I the Lord your God am a jealous God, visiting the iniquity of the fathers on the children to the third and fourth generation of those that hate me, but showing steadfast love to thousands of those who love me and keep my commandments. You shall not take the name of the Lord your God in vain, for the Lord will not hold him guiltless who takes his name in vain."

Commentary

You will have noticed that the first commandment mentions "other gods". When the Jews settled in Canaan, in the thirteenth century BCE, the Canaanites (and those in neighbouring countries) worshipped other gods such as Ashur, Ishtar, Marduk and Baal. It was an era of polytheism.

Some of the Jews also paid homage to these Semitic gods, to the chagrin of the scribes who made it crystal clear that the Hebrew God was supreme—an all-powerful, watchful, and jealous God. Jews who worshiped other gods would incur His wrath—idolaters would be punished and so would their children and their children's children.

Thus, the first three commandments may be viewed as a prologue—one that sets a tone of awe and fear for the seven commandments that follow.

COMMANDMENT # 4

"Remember the Sabbath day, to keep it holy. Six days you shall labour, and do all your work, but the seventh day is a Sabbath to the Lord your God. On it you shall not do any work, you, or your son, or your daughter, your male servant, or your female servant."

As with the first three commandments, there were severe consequences for Jews who broke the Sabbath Law. "Moses assembled all the congregation of the people of Israel and said to them.... For six days shall work be done, but on the seventh day you shall have a Sabbath of solemn rest, holy to the Lord. Whoever does any work on it shall be put to death. You shall kindle no fire in all your dwelling places on the Sabbath day" (Exodus 35:1-3).

Commentary

Apart from the threat of death and the injunction not to light a fireplace even on a cold, miserable day, the fourth commandment makes perfect sense. To work from dawn to dusk seven days a week is foolish and heartless. Bodies and minds work better and last longer when people can rest and recharge their batteries.

COMMANDMENT # 5

"Honour your father and your mother, that your days may be long in the land which the Lord your God is giving you".

Commentary

I'm sure you noticed the incentive for honouring parents— "that your days may be long". I would hope we would honour our parents, not for longevity, but because we love them and are grateful for all they have done for us.

My main concern with this fifth commandment is its omission of any exceptions. Are we to honour a parent who is physically and emotionally abusive to us? Are we to honour a parent who screams threats at his or her partner and who also is physically violent? Are we to honour a parent who drinks or gambles so that there is not enough money for clothes, or food or rent?

COMMANDMENT # 6

"You shall not murder".

Commentary

This sixth commandment seems clear and logical, but there are many instances in the Bible when murder was sanctioned. God drowned all of earth's inhabitants except for Noah and his family. He also rained down fire and brimstone on all the adults, children, and animals in the cities of Sodom and Gomorrah.

Nor did this injunction apply to Moses when he descended from the mountain and discovered that some of his people were worshipping a golden calf. Enraged he ordered the execution of three thousand men, even though they had not yet seen or heard this sixth commandment (Exodus 32:27-28). Nor did this commandment apply to Joshua, the military leader who allegedly wiped out the seven indigenous Semitic tribes that occupied the promised land of Canaan (Joshua 8-12).

COMMANDMENT #7

"You shall not commit adultery".

Commentary

In biblical times men could have a second wife as well as concubines and female slaves. (Not a great era for women.)

COMMANDMENT #8

"You shall not steal".

The Ten Commandments

Commentary

The consequences for theft were severe. If you stole your neighbour's ox and were caught, you were to return five oxen to your neighbour. If you failed to make restitution, you could be sold into slavery. (See Exodus 22:1-4.)

Some 21ˢᵗ century countries such as Saudi Arabia have even more stringent consequences for stealing, but I digress.

COMMANDMENT #9

"You shall not bear false witness against your neighbour".

Commentary

(Amen.)

COMMANDMENT #10

"You shall not covet your neighbour's house; you shall not covet your neighbour's wife, or his male servant, or his female servant, or his ox, or his donkey, or anything that is your neighbour's".

Commentary

It is important to note that a male servant was not a butler, nor was a female servant a hired maid. They were slaves. In this commandment they, along with the neighbour's wife and animals, were categorized as property.

To covet means to want, to long for, or to desire. This last commandment is, unfortunately, beyond the grasp of most mortal beings. Who amongst us has not been envious of the homes of neighbours, or their new cars, or their clothing, or

their green, weed-free lawns, or their well-mannered, clever
children? Sometimes envy works to our advantage. I'm sure
there have been times in your life when you worked harder
to get better results at school and at work—thanks to a
little envy.

A Concluding Thought

While I appreciate the importance of laws forbidding murder,
adultery, theft, lying and envy, I wish there had been several
additional laws to protect the rights of children, and women.

✍ Author's Note

Heaven, in the cosmology of the Sumerians, Greeks, Romans, and
Hebrews, was always **up** so that the nearest you could get to the gods
would be at the top of a mountain. Commandments given by the gods
had more authority than those given by priests or monarchs. Thus, the
scribe who recorded the Ten Commandments in the sixth century BCE
was following an ancient precedent when he claimed that God had given
Moses the Ten Commandments from a mountain top.

When you study Near Eastern History, you learn that other societies
had codes of conduct recorded long before the biblical account of Moses
coming down from a mountain with stone tablets from God. Following
are three ancient codes.

THE CODE OF KING UR-NAMMU (C.2112-2095 BCE)

The oldest code of laws yet discovered, written on clay tablets in
Sumerian cuneiform, is that of Ur-Nammu. Fragments of this code
were found in the cities of Nippur and Ur and are now stored in the
Archaeology Museums of Istanbul. Translated in 1965, we have forty of
their fifty-seven laws. Some of the laws prohibited usury, theft, murder,

and the seizure of people's property and persons. Other laws limited the power of priests and wealthy property owners in order to protect widows and orphans. Although murder, robbery, adultery and rape were capital offenses, some of the punishments called for fines rather than an "eye for an eye" retribution. If you would like to read some of these ancient laws, see Addendum D.

THE CODE OF KING HAMMURABI (18ᵀᴴ CENTURY BCE)

Three hundred years later, c.1760 BCE, in the reign of the Babylonian King Hammurabi, another ancient law code was inscribed on a beautiful, black basalt stele discovered at Susa, in what is now SW Iran. It can be viewed at the Louvre in Paris. It should come as no surprise to us that according to the inscription, Hammurabi received his laws on a mountain top from the sun god, Shamash. His code covers many topics such as slavery, slander, theft, trade and divorce. Some of the penalties were more stringent than those of Ur-Nammu. If you use a search engine, you can find the 282 laws that make up the Code of Hammurabi.

THE PAPYRUS OF THE THEBAN SCRIBE
ANI (13ᵀᴴ CENTURY BCE)

This Egyptian funeral text, written in hieroglyphic script on papyrus, was found in the tomb of Ani, and is now preserved in the British Museum of London. (Sir Wallis Budge admitted stealing it from an Egyptian warehouse!) The text, dated to c.1250 BCE, reiterates a common belief in the New Kingdom of Egypt (1555-1077 BCE) that the deceased would be judged by Osiris in the hereafter for any wrongdoings in his earthly life. Thus, Ani, before being admitted to the afterlife, was required to recite the "Negative Confession" which details the moral behaviour expected from him by the gods. These confessions are found on pages 347-349 of *The Egyptian Book of the Dead* by E.A. Wallis Budge, plates XXXI to

XXXIII. Each confession is addressed to an Egyptian god. Following are eight confessions.

+ I have not stolen (plate # 3).
+ I have done no murder (4).
+ I have spoken no lies (8).
+ I have not committed fornication (11).
+ I have not been angry and wrathful except justly (19).
+ I have not acted with insolence (28).
+ I have not judged hastily (30).
+ I have never cursed God (37).

You might wonder how Jewish scribes could have known of these "Negative Confessions" found in Egypt. It is not a mystery. We know from archaeologists that in the Bronze Age (c.3200 to 1200 BCE) Egypt's power and influence extended far beyond its borders. In this era there was a significant Egyptian presence in Canaan, Babylon, and Assyria. For example, the Armana letters detail some of the commerce that existed between Egypt and Canaan.

These clay tablets, discovered in Upper Egypt at Armana, are archives of diplomatic correspondence between Egyptian administrators and their representatives in Canaan during the reign of Akhenaton and Amenhotep III in the 14th century BCE. The letters were written in Akkadian cuneiform, the language used in ancient Mesopotamia. For additional evidence of Egypt's presence in Canaan, see my notes on the Merneptah stele in Addendum E. The inscription shows that Canaan was a vassal possession of Egypt.

Commentary

It is reasonable to assume that the Hebrew scribes who included the Ten Commandments in the O.T. would have been familiar with earlier Near Eastern codes of morality, and that these codes influenced what they wrote. When the Jewish scholar, Samuel Noah Kramer died on November 26,

1990, he was a world-renowned expert in Sumerian history and language. He concluded that Sumerian literature left "its deep impression on Hebrews". (See pg. 55 "History Begins at Sumer").

Professors Andrew Hill and John Walton, of Wheaton College, also acknowledged the influence of earlier codes of law when they wrote, "The influence of the ancient Near Eastern legal tradition on the form and function of Hebrew law is undeniable and widely documented." (See pg. 52 of "A Survey of the Old Testament" published in 2000.)

I included this latter quotation because Wheaton College is a conservative Christian college that esteems the Bible as the inerrant Word of God. Nevertheless, these two professors acknowledged the influence "of the ancient Near Eastern legal tradition" on Hebrew law.

CHAPTER 7

The Torah (Law)

WHEN YOU READ the Torah, you may feel overwhelmed and occasionally appalled. By the Torah I am referring to the 613 laws found in the Books of Genesis, Exodus, Leviticus, Numbers and Deuteronomy. I'd be surprised if you have read these laws, and I don't mean that as a criticism. Why would you need to know how to cut up and sacrifice a bull? Why would you need to know which vestments Levite priests were supposed to wear 2,600 years ago?

The Torah has been aptly described as a "forest of details" covering a wide spectrum of topics such as the following:

- Moral laws: murder, theft, honesty and adultery.
- Social laws: property, inheritance, marriage and divorce.
- Food laws: what is clean and unclean, cooking and storing food.
- Purity laws: involving menstruation, skin diseases, seminal emissions, and deformities.
- Feasts: the Day of Atonement, Passover, Feast of Tabernacles.
- Sacrifices: the sin offering, Passover sacrifice, etc.
- Offerings: burnt offering, whole offering, peace offering, etc.
- Instructions for the priesthood and the high priest.
- Instructions for the Tabernacle and the Temple in Jerusalem.

When you read these ancient rules and regulations, you get some idea of what life was like in Canaan 2,600 years ago in a theocracy when priests determined their civil and religious laws. Later in my commentary, you will see how the priests justified and enforced these laws.

As you read the Torah, you will have questions. Why were the Hebrews allowed to eat locusts, grasshoppers and crickets but not shrimp or lobster? Why were animals that did not chew the cud "detestable"? Did they really put to death a son or daughter for cursing a parent? Did they stone to death those who were mediums or wizards? Did fathers sell daughters into slavery as sanctioned in Leviticus 21:7? Why was there no mention of selling sons into slavery?

You will notice that in some of the laws women were appallingly misunderstood and woefully treated. A menstruating woman was deemed "unclean" for seven days and anyone who touched her (even inadvertently) was unclean until the evening. When she was married, she was expected to be a virgin, but there was no such requirement for her fiancé. If "tokens of her virginity" were missing on her first night of marriage, she could be stoned to death (See Deuteronomy 22:20-21). A woman who gave birth to a boy was considered unclean for seven days and not allowed into the sanctuary for an additional thirty-three days. If the new-born was a girl, the mother was unclean for fourteen days and not permitted to enter the sanctuary for an additional sixty-six days. Once these days of "purification" had passed, new mothers had to make a sin offering for atonement.

[I know you are wondering what sin they had committed. So am I.]

DIETARY RULES

The dietary rules in Leviticus Chapter 11 are complex and perplexing. Following are the basic rules for kosher—food that meets the requirement of Jewish law. "Whatever parts the hoof and is cloven-footed and chews the cud, among the animals, you may eat." This "hoof" definition excluded all animals with paws (including predators like wolves and lions) as well as animals such as pigs, camels, rabbits, and snakes. Fish were on the menu but only those that had "fins and scales". These two prerequisites excluded such creatures of the sea as shrimp, lobsters, oysters, clams, crabs, and octopuses. Insects that went on all fours were "detestable" except those that used their legs to leap such as crickets and grasshoppers. Those the Hebrews could eat.

Dairy products were problematic. They could be eaten, but not in combination with meat products. This prohibition is based on three identical verses found in Exodus 23:19, 34:26, and Deuteronomy 14:21. "You shall not boil a young goat in its mother's milk."

If you are confused by these laws, keep reading because there are explanations for the Jewish dietary laws to which I have referred.

Commentary

Dr. Mary Douglas, an English anthropologist, offered an interesting explanation of the dietary laws based on Genesis 1:9. "Let the waters under the heavens be gathered together into one place, and let the dry land appear." She theorized that the priests had interpreted this verse to mean, first of all, that God had divided the world into three divisions: the waters, the sky and the dry land. Second, they concluded that God intended the animals in these three areas to be distinct and separate. Creatures that were a mixture of these separate divisions were hybrids, and were not to be eaten.

For example, lobsters with their legs and claws lived in the sea but lacked fins and scales. Thus lobsters were a forbidden hybrid as were crocodiles because they walked on land with legs and yet lived in water. Seals could not be eaten because they lived on land and sea, and most importantly, lacked fins and scales. Nor was it kosher to eat birds such as storks because they stood and hunted for long periods standing in water. Seagulls also spent much of their time swimming and hunting in water. I have trouble understanding why birds such as falcons were excluded; perhaps it was their predatory nature that made them "detestable".

Douglas' theory is plausible but her interpretation of Genesis 1:9 seems to be contradicted by the creation story in Genesis 1:25; namely, on the sixth day after God created the beasts of the earth, He "saw that it was good". If all the animals were initially "good", why would God change his mind and later declare (by Moses according to the Torah) that some animals were "detestable"? The details of Douglas' theory are found in "Purity and Danger" written in 1966 and published by Rutledge, London, U.K.

Interestingly, in a 2002 revision of "Purity and Danger", Douglas in the preface retracted her explanation of kosher rules. She called it "a major mistake". She concluded that the Israelites could only eat animals that were allowed to be sacrificed, animals that depended on herdsmen. These were "clean" animals. All other animals were an abomination to eat, but were not "impure."

Others have speculated that there may have been medical reasons for banning certain foods such as lobsters, shrimp and pigs. Lobsters can spoil quickly, especially in warm weather. People can get hepatitis from shellfish caught in waters polluted by sewage. If you eat under-cooked pork, you could become infected with trichinosis—a nasty disease caused by parasitic, hair-like worms. This hypothesis may have some basis because the underlying assumption is that those who wrote the laws of kosher realized that there was an association between diet and specific illnesses. It is an interesting conjecture.

Others have suggested that the early Hebrews banned pigs for hygienic reasons. Pigs will eat anything including faeces and rotting meat, and they love to wallow in mud (to minimize sunburn). Perhaps the Hebrew priests found them revolting because they believed cleanliness was a virtue of paramount importance. When you read the Book of Leviticus, you see that the priests were obsessed with cleanliness. Is this why the pig was so detestable to the Lord?

American anthropologist Marvin Harris posed a pragmatic reason to explain the taboo on pork. He pointed out that raising pigs was not cost-effective. They required lots of water, shade, and grain—resources that were often scarce in the Middle East. Nor did pigs provide milk. In his opinion, it made more sense for farmers to raise animals like goats, sheep and cattle.

The late Christopher Hitchens also waded into the dietary debate with these astute observations: a pig's DNA is so similar to ours that we can receive transplants of heart valves, skin and kidneys from "this fine beast"; the shriek of a pig about to be slaughtered or being neutered is disturbingly "human"; many firemen will not eat pork because the smell of a roasting pig reminds them of disastrous house fires; Hawaiian cannibals were known to refer to their human sacrifices as "long pig" due to the similarity to pork. (See "God Is Not Great" pages 37-41.)

As previously mentioned, the Torah forbids cooking milk in combination with meat. A great deal of debate has ensued over this rule for centuries. Today Orthodox Jews take extreme steps to follow Exodus 23:19, "You shall not boil a young goat in its mother's milk". Their kosher kitchen must have two separate sets of cooking utensils, dishes, and cutlery—one for meat and one for milk (which also includes eggs and cheese). You must wait six hours after eating meat before eating dairy products! I have researched a number of internet sites to read rabbinical explanations of these kosher requirements. Maybe I'm thick-headed, but I still don't get it.

The last point for you to consider is that the 613 laws that make up the Torah established a unique cultural identity for the Jewish people. Their dietary and ritual rules were markedly different from those of neighbouring tribes and nations. If followed, these laws negated or minimized social interactions with other tribes. This raises the question of how the priests motivated their people to follow these laws which were distinctly different from those of other nations.

I put the onus on the priests because their form of government was a theocracy. Whether or not they were "ruled" by judges or monarchs, the Levites (their priests) held the reins of power and they used this power to enforce the keeping of the Torah. They did so at times by bribes and threats. For example, in chapter twenty-eight of Deuteronomy, we find thirteen verses that describe blessings from God for obedience, and fifty-four verses that describe dire consequences for those who disobey God's laws.

"And if you faithfully obey the voice of the Lord your God, being careful to do all his commandments that I command you today, the Lord your God will set you high above all the nations of the earth. And all these blessings shall come upon you . . . . Blessed shall be the fruit of your womb and the fruit of your ground and the fruit of your cattle, and increase of your herds and the young of your flock . . . . The Lord will cause your enemies who rise against you to be defeated before you . . . And the Lord will make you abound in prosperity . . . . And you shall lend to many nations, but you shall not borrow."

"But if you will not obey the voice of the Lord your God or be careful to do all his commandments and his statutes that I command you today, then all these curses shall come upon you and overtake you . . . . The Lord will send on you curses, confusion, and frustration in all that you undertake to do, until you are destroyed and perish quickly . . . . The Lord will strike you with wasting disease and with fever, inflammation, and fiery heat, and with drought and with blight and with mildew . . . . The Lord will cause you to be defeated before your enemies." The threats go on and on. There are over fifty curses.

In the introduction of this chapter, I wrote that women were "appallingly misunderstood and woefully treated". It is sad but obvious that those who wrote about "menstrual uncleanness" were ignorant of a woman's physiology and particularly her reproductive organs. They thought that if a woman were barren, it was either her fault or God had made her so, usually as a punishment.

We saw this masculine bias earlier in Genesis. In the second story of creation, God made woman _last_ because Adam was lonely and needed a helpmate. When Adam and Eve were driven out of the Garden of Eden, it was mainly Eve's fault for enticing Adam to eat the forbidden fruit. This act of disobedience was the "original sin" for which Eve and her daughters were to be punished in all future generations with mortality and painful childbirths.

For additional examples of the mistreatment of women in the O.T., you can use a search engine to check out SAB, Women (Skeptics Annotated Bible). This site quotes many verses from Genesis to Malachi to show the mistreatment of wives and daughters. For example, men's names are recorded frequently throughout the O.T. but that is not the case with the names of wives and daughters. Also, when scribes traced the genealogy of important leaders, they only listed male names. Men, in Deuteronomy 16:16 were required to attend three religious feasts every year, but no such demand was made of women. Polygamy was widely practiced in the O.T. as was the right of men to have concubines and female slaves.

Biblical apologists may say that I have taken verses out of context, that I have unfairly judged an early Hebrew society from my twenty-first century perspective, that other Near Eastern cultures treated women similarly, that God had his reasons for the laws he gave through Moses, and that I should not question his wisdom. If they are right in this admonishment, I can look forward to a fiery future.

Elizabeth Cody Stanton (1815-1902), an American suffragist and social activist, had no qualms about questioning the God of the O.T. and the Torah. I will end this chapter with two of her quotations.

"The Bible teaches that woman brought sin and death into the world, that she precipitated the fall of the race, and that she was arraigned before the judgment seat of Heaven, tried, condemned and sentenced. Marriage for her was to be a condition of bondage, maternity a period of suffering and anguish, and in silence and subjection, she was to play the role of a dependant on man's bounty for all her material wants, and for all the information she might desire on the vital questions of the hour, she was commanded to ask her husband at home. Here is the Bible position of woman briefly summed up" (From The Woman's Bible).

"We hold these truths to be self-evident: that all men and women are created equal" (From History of Woman Suffrage).

✎ Author's Note

The status of Jewish women today is VERY different. Jewish women in the 21ˢᵗ century are not uneducated, submissive, subordinate or inferior. If you research "Rabbi Women", you will see the important roles and contributions of Jewish women in synagogues and communities.

CHAPTER 8

The Judges

(c. 1300 to 1000 BCE)

~~~~~~~~~~

W E NOW RETURN to our epic narrative. We have looked at the creation of the cosmos, the first humans (Adam and Eve), the Patriarchs, Moses, the Exodus, and the Torah. In chapter five we reviewed the conquest of Canaan, the "Promised Land". The Book of Joshua gave a detailed list of the cities, kings and tribes that were defeated by the forces of Joshua. They killed all their enemies including women and children. "So Joshua took the whole land, according to all that the Lord had spoken to Moses. And Joshua gave it for an inheritance to Israel according to their tribal allotments. And the land had rest from war" (Joshua 11:23).

Now we come to the Book of Judges which covers 300 years from the time the Hebrews entered Canaan to the reign of King Saul. Although there was no central government in this era, the Hebrew tribes appointed judges to settle disputes and to keep some semblance of order and unity. Only fourteen judges are mentioned, so consequently we only have brief accounts of what happened in this time-frame. What we find in the Book of Judges are some interesting and bizarre anecdotes involving treachery, murder, misogamy, and a war that almost wiped out the tribe of Benjamin.

Commentary

As you read the Book of Judges, you realize that the enemies defeated by Joshua were not annihilated because the wars in Canaan continued. How do we reconcile these contradictory accounts? One possible explanation is that the scribes used different texts and oral traditions—sources that were sometimes contradictory. The most plausible explanation is that with the passage of time, the conquest and settlement of Canaan became a vague, disjointed memory. The Book of Judges was compiled in the sixth century BCE, many centuries after the Hebrews settled in Canaan. Another factor is that the authors of Judges were not historians; they were scribes who were more concerned with religious issues than with historical accuracy.

We have already seen one of their agendas—to give their citizens an epic history, one that would remind them of a special relationship with God that went back to the Patriarchs and to Moses, one that would inspire them to keep the Torah and the customs and traditions of their forefathers.

They also needed a history that would explain why the "chosen people of God", who had been promised possession of the land of Canaan, had to fight so often for their survival in Canaan. In the Book of Judges the answer is clear. When the Hebrews failed to follow the Torah or, worst of all, when they worshiped other gods, they suffered dire consequences. God, however, could be appeased by pleas and burnt offerings. Thus throughout the Book of Judges we find a repetitive cycle of idolatry, divine punishment, repentance and deliverance.

Anecdotes are an integral part of the Book of Judges. Some of them might have been oral traditions handed down through many generations. These stories kept alive the names of some of the judges—heroes as well as villains as we shall see. I have included summaries of seven of their judges—Ehud,

Deborah, Gideon, Abimelech, Jephthah, Samson, and the last judge, Samuel.

EHUD

Ehud, the second judge, persuaded Eglon (an obese king of Moab) to meet for a private conversation without the presence of attendants and guards. Then "Ehud reached with his left hand, took the sword from his right thigh, and thrust it into Eglon's belly. And the hilt also went in after the blade, and the fat closed over the blade, for he did not draw the sword out of his belly." Following his escape from the king's inner chamber, Ehud and his forces seized the fords of the river Jordan. "And they killed at that time about 10,000 of the Moabites, all strong able-bodied men; not a man escaped." (Judges 3)

DEBORAH

The only female judge mentioned was Deborah, a prophetess. She and her general, Barak, led an army of 10,000 Hebrews against the Canaanite commander, Sisera (Judges 4). "And the Lord routed Sisera and all his chariots and all his army . . . not a man was left." Sisera escaped, however, and took refuge in the tent of Jael, the wife of Heber. When the exhausted Sisera fell asleep, Jael took a tent peg and drove it into his temple. Jael's deed is glorified in Judges 5:1-31 in a Song of Victory sung by Barak and Deborah.

GIDEON

Gideon, a man of great valor, was one of the most famous of the judges. Following the directives of the Lord, he whittled down his army from

22,000 to 300 warriors and with this force he defeated a Midianite army of 120,000 without losing a man (Judges 7).

ABIMELECH

Although Gideon had seventy sons from his wives and concubines, he chose Abimelech, the son of one of his unnamed concubines, to be his successor. As the newly appointed judge, Abimelech consolidated his position by executing all but one of his seventy brothers.

When the city of Shechem opposed his rule, he "captured the city and killed the people that were in it, and he razed the city and sowed it with salt." After a thousand of the survivors took refuge in the Tower of Shechem, Abimelech had his men piled brushwood against the stronghold and burned to death all those inside. He attempted to do the same to those who fled to the Tower of Thebez, but his plans were thwarted by a woman who threw down a millstone which struck him on the head. Mortally wounded, he summoned his armour-bearer, and said to him, "Draw your sword and kill me, lest they say of me, a woman killed him" (Judges 9:54).

JEPHTHAH

The ninth judge was Jephthah, the son of a harlot. Although spurned by his family, the elders of Gilead pleaded with this "mighty" warrior to lead their forces against the Ammonites. So Jephthah made a vow to the Lord, "If you will give the Ammonites into my hand, then whoever comes out from the doors of my house to meet me when I return in peace from the Ammonites shall be the Lord's, and I will offer it up as a burnt offering" (Judges 11:30-31). To his great chagrin, the first to greet him after he slaughtered the inhabitants of twenty Ammonite cities was his daughter, his only child. After allowing his daughter two months to mourn her virginity, Jephthah kept his vow. She was sacrificed to the Lord as a burnt offering.

SAMSON

The most famous of the judges was Samson a man of prodigious strength who was said to have killed a lion with his bare hands and a thousand Philistines with the jawbone of an ass. He judged Israel for twenty years. One of his wives was Delilah, a Philistine. Using her feminine guiles, she eventually discovered the secret of his strength—his long uncut hair. While he slept, she cut his locks and turned him over to her country-men, the Philistines, who seized him, gouged out his eyes, and impris-oned him.

Samson got his revenge when he was brought to a house where they made "sport" of him. Standing between two pillars, Samson (whose hair had grown back while in prison) pushed against the pillars and brought the whole house crashing down, killing more than those he had ever killed before in his life. We are told there were 3,000 Philistines on the roof of the house (16:27)!

Commentary

No archaeological or external historical records exist to confirm the wars described in the Book of Judges. The numbers of those who fought in battles and the numbers killed are greatly exaggerated—if, in fact, these events occurred. If Gideon, with only an army of 300 men, had wiped out an army of 120,000, there should have been some physical evi-dence of this mayhem, but there is no corroborating evidence. Time and the retelling of such stories resulted in grandiose numbers that defy reason—such as Samson killing a thou-sand Philistines with the jawbone of a donkey.

The status and treatment of women is another theme we find in the Book of Judges. You may have noticed how seldom women are named in this book, unless you slay an enemy in a spectacular manner or are an esteemed prophetess who becomes one of the judges. Husbands, with a few exceptions, were more important than their wives.

In Judges chapter 19, there is a gruesome story of a Levite travelling with his concubine. When they arrived at Gibeah, a city of the tribe of Benjamin, an old man took them to his home for the night. While eating supper, the men of the city banged on the door and demanded that the old man turn over the male guest so that they might "know" him. (This is a biblical euphemism for sex.) The old man refused. To save his male guest, he shoved a daughter and the concubine out the door. "Behold, here are my virgin daughter and his concubine. Let me bring them out now. Violate them and do with them what seems good to you" (19:24). The next morning the Levite discovered his concubine lying on the doorstep—dead. Sadly, misogyny was alive and well in the minds of the scribes responsible for the Book of Judges.

This shocking story is important because it explains why the tribe of Benjamin almost vanished. The Levite tied the body of his dead concubine on the back of his donkey and took her home where he divided her corpse into twelve pieces, which he sent to the tribes of Israel. Thus motivated to avenge her death, the Israelites mustered a large force of armed men and attacked both the Benjaminites who had come to defend the city and the inhabitants of Gibeah. When the carnage ended, 40,000 Israelites were dead along with those who lived in Gibeah, and over 25,000 of the tribe of Benjamin. Only 600 men of the tribe of Benjamin survived.

Because the tribe of Benjamin was deemed to be responsible for this whole debacle, the other tribes of Israel swore a sacred vow not to allow their daughters to marry into

Benjamin's tribe. If the 600 survivors had no wives, the whole tribe would die out. It was a dilemma that needed to be solved. The Israelites resolved the conundrum by attacking a town called Jabesh-gilead because the inhabitants had refused to join the coalition in taking vengeance against the tribe of Benjamin. With a force of 12,000 men, they killed everyone except for 400 virgins who were given to the surviving 600 men.

As more wives were still needed, the elders came up with a cunning plan. They advised those without wives to hide in the vineyards close to a yearly feast that took place at Shiloh and to snatch young girls who came to dance. Thus the tribe of Benjamin was saved.

SAMUEL—THE LAST JUDGE (1 SAMUEL CHAPTERS 1- 8)

Even before he was born, Samuel was destined for greatness. Hannah, his mother, had no children "because the Lord had closed her womb." Her prayer for a son was answered and so, keeping her vow, she gave her three-year-old son to be raised by Eli, the priest. As a boy, one night Samuel heard the voice of God calling his name. In the morning he reluctantly informed Eli that he had heard these words, "I am about to punish Eli's house forever . . . because his sons were blaspheming God, and he did not restrain them." Thus Eli knew that Yahweh had chosen the boy Samuel to be a prophet—to communicate the Word of God to the Hebrews.

Samuel grew up in an era dominated by the Philistines, an era where Canaanites worshipped such gods as Dagon, Baal and Ashtaroth. Under Samuel's leadership the children of Israel repented of their idolatry and worshiped only Yahweh. "And the hand of the Lord was against the Philistines all the days of Samuel. The cities that the Philistines had taken from Israel were restored to Israel" (7:13-14).

Samuel was praised for administering justice, but there was a problem of succession because the people of Israel distrusted Samuel's sons. The people clamored for a king. "Behold, you are old and your sons do not walk in your ways. Now appoint for us a king to govern us like all the nations" (8:5).

After praying for guidance, Samuel heard these words from Yahweh. "Obey the voice of the people in all that they say to you; for they have not rejected you, but they have rejected me from being king over them." Samuel conceded to their wishes, but first he warned them that life under a monarchy would be fraught with negatives: their young men would be conscripted for military service; their daughters would have to serve as cooks; the king would take a tenth of all they grew. They would be slaves of their monarch.

Commentary

Samuel could do no wrong. Nowhere is he criticized even when he advised King Saul to slaughter the Amaleks. "Now go and smite Amalek and devote to destruction all that they have. Do not spare them, but kill both man and woman, child and infant, ox and sheep, camel and donkey" (1 Samuel 15:3).

What we find in Judges are two conflicting ideologies. There were those who wanted a king and those who preferred a theocracy—government by God through priests like Samuel. It was difficult, however, for priests to administer justice to the scattered nomadic tribes of the Hebrews. Nor were the priests able to unify the tribes against powerful enemies like the Philistines. The last verse of Judges paints a succinct picture of the problem: "In those days there was no king in Israel; every man did what was right in his own eyes."

This verse reflected the opinion of those who favoured the reign of kings and who saw the era of David and Solomon as Israel's greatest historical period. Other scribes disagreed. As they looked back at this era from their sixth century BCE perspective, they saw this period as Israel's greatest mistake. Consequently, they included stories to show the moral ineptness of their kings.

Were they heroes or villains? As you read the next chapter, you will have the opportunity to formulate your answer.

CHAPTER 9

The Monarchy Period of Saul, David and Solomon

(c. 1012 BCE to 925 BCE)

~~~~~~~~~~

W E HAVE NO external evidence, outside of the Old Testament, of the Exodus, the Conquest of Canaan and the Judges. We have no clay tablets or inscribed monuments that refer to these eras or to key figures such as Moses and Joshua. As we turn to the monarchy era, however, we do have two brief references from archaeology that confirm that there was a "House of David". See Addendum E for a description of the Dan Stele and the Bubastite Relief at Karnak, Egypt.

***

Most nations have a period in their history that they recall with pride—eras of prestige, power and prosperity. Egypt reached its prominence in the New Kingdom Era during the reigns of the Rameses from c.1550 BCE to 1077 BCE. The Greeks enjoyed a Golden Age in the fifth century BCE. The Jews too have an historical period that they recall with pride and nostalgia. Some of the scribes responsible for the narrative we have been studying saw the reigns of Saul, David, and particularly that of Solomon, as their Golden Age. It was a time when the tribes in the north (Israel) and the south (Judah) united as one nation and broke free from the dominance of their neighbours. It was during this era of power and prosperity that Solomon built the Temple of Jerusalem.

The main books that depict this era are those of Samuel, Kings and Chronicles. If you read these texts expecting an orderly, chronological history of people and events, you will be disappointed. What you find is a collection of anecdotes, annals, and several long lists of names that can cure insomnia. The anecdotes, however, will keep you awake—stories of assassinations, intrigues, competing coronations, adultery, murder and incest.

KING SAUL (C.1012-1005) (1 SAMUEL)

The prophet Samuel called all the Hebrew tribes together to meet their demands for a king. By lot it was determined that the king should come from the tribe of Benjamin. (Lots could be sticks with markings, or stones with symbols.) Again, by lot, they chose the Matrite family. In this family there was one "taller than any of the people from the shoulders upwards". His name was Saul, "chosen by the Lord" as the first king of the Hebrews.

After Saul became king, he defeated all his enemies—Moab, the Ammonites, Edom, the kings of Zobah, and the Philistines. "Wherever he turned he routed them. And he did valiantly and struck the Amalekites and delivered Israel out of the hands of those who plundered them" (14:48).

Saul was praised as a great military leader even though he suffered from some form of mental affliction. "Now the spirit of the Lord departed from Saul, and a harmful spirit from the Lord tormented him" (16:14). Ironically, it was the shepherd lad, David, who was summoned to play his lyre and calm the king. This is the same David who later slew Goliath, scattered the Philistines and became a popular hero. "Saul has struck down his thousands and David his ten thousands" (18:7).

This mantra made Saul so jealous that on several occasions he tried to kill David. Even Jonathon, Saul's son, helped David to escape the wrath of his father. Ahimelech, a high priest of Nob, a place near Jerusalem, also befriended and protected David. He paid dearly for this perceived lack of loyalty. Saul attacked Nob. In the massacre that followed, he killed Ahimelech, eighty-five priests, and all the inhabitants and animals in the city. To escape from Saul, David fled to the land of the Philistines where he formed an alliance with Achish, the son of a Philistine king. Here he was safe—along with six hundred of his men, their wives and children.

In the last days of his reign, Saul faced a formidable army of the Philistines. Fearing for his life, he sought guidance from the Lord by the Urim (a priestly device for receiving oracles), and by prophets, but Saul received no spiritual guidance, not even by dreams. Consequently, Saul sought out a medium even though they were condemned and forbidden in the Torah (Leviticus 20:27).

The medium summoned up the spirit of Samuel. Disgruntled at being disturbed, Samuel (an old man wrapped in a robe) gave this ominous prediction: "Because you did not obey the voice of the Lord and did not carry out his fierce wrath against Amalek, therefore the Lord has done this thing to you this day. Moreover, the Lord will give Israel also with you into the hand of the Philistines, and tomorrow you and your sons will be with me. The Lord will give the army of Israel also into the hand of the Philistines" (1 Samuel 28:18-19).

These prophecies came true. Three of his sons died in the battle and Saul was grievously wounded. Rather than be captured, Saul died ignominiously by deliberately falling upon his own sword. "So Saul died for his breach of faith. . . . he did not keep the command of the Lord, and also consulted a medium, seeking guidance. Therefore the Lord put him to death and turned the kingdom over to David the son of Jesse." (1 Chronicles 10:13-14)

Commentary

As noted in the last chapter, some of the scribes preferred a theocracy to a monarchy. This preference helps explain why the author of 1 Samuel turned a negative spotlight on the reign of Saul. To discredit Saul as a vengeful, vindictive leader, the author included the story of Ahimelech, the priest of Nob who had protected David. To punish Ahimelech, Saul attacked Nob and killed the high priest Ahimelech, eighty-five priests, and all the inhabitants and animals in the city. You can sense the scribe's contempt of Saul as he described the massacre at Nob, and Saul's jealous rages.

Although the scribe could not ignore his military achievements, he had no reservations in detailing additional flaws and mistakes. We learn that Saul offended God on two occasions. First, just before a crucial battle, he offered a sacrifice to God instead of waiting for the prophet Samuel to carry out this priestly function.

Second, Saul failed to carry out God's commandment to slaughter all the Amalekites and all their livestock. Although he did kill all the women, infants and children, Saul spared their king, Agag, and allowed his men to keep the best of the animals. Samuel was angry. "Why then did you not obey the word of the Lord? Why did you swoop on the spoil, and do what was evil in the sight of the Lord?" After chastising Saul, Samuel "hacked Agag to pieces before the Lord in Gilgal" (15:33).

This story must be disconcerting for those who believe that every word in the Bible is "the Word of God". Did the Lord command Saul to slaughter all the Amalekites and their livestock? Was the Lord pleased that Samuel hacked Agag to pieces?

The scribe responsible for 1 Samuel thought that the Temple of Jerusalem should be the centre for worshipping and for making sacrifices to Yahweh. Understandably, these priestly goals were not shared by the Jews who lived in the northern settlements of Israel and who had their own shrines "in the high places" for worship and sacrifice.

As instructed by God, the prophet Samuel chose and anointed David, the youthful son of Jesse, to succeed King Saul. "Now he was ruddy and had beautiful eyes and was handsome (1 Samuel 16:12)". Renowned for his musical talents, David played his lyre and calmed and comforted Saul when he was tormented by an evil spirit sent by the Lord. "And David came to Saul, and entered his service. And Saul loved him greatly, and he became his armour bearer (I Samuel 16:21)".

David was also renowned for his courage having killed lions and bears as a shepherd. Although not trained as a warrior, he volunteered to fight a giant Philistine called Goliath because no one else in the Israelite army would accept the challenge. Armed only with his slingshot, he fought Goliath whose height was said to be six cubits and a span. (A cubit is sixteen to twenty inches and a span is nine inches.) This giant, who was at least eight feet tall, was a formidable opponent, but David killed him with his slingshot, and then used Goliath's sword to decapitate him. This feat galvanized the Israelite forces to slaughter the fleeing Philistines. Soon afterwards Saul appointed David to lead his forces—not one of his own sons.

In time Saul became insanely jealous of David's military successes and his growing popularity. On at least two occasions he tried to spear David. Saul came up with a devious plan to have David killed in battle. He offered his daughter Michal to David asking ONLY for a hundred foreskins of the Philistines as the marriage present. This plot failed because David and his men killed two hundred of the enemy, and so David married Michal. Though David was now the son-in-law of the king, he was still perceived as a threat and an enemy. Warned and aided by his wife, Michal, and his friend Jonathan, David fled to escape the wrath of Saul. As punishment Saul banished Michal from his presence and sent her away to be the wife of Palti.

Eventually David, along with 600 of his men (and their wives and children), found safety in the land of the Philistines and lived in a town called Ziklag. From there David and his men made frequent raids against the Geshurites, the Girzites, and the Amalakites. "And David would strike the land, and would leave neither man nor woman alive, but would take away the sheep, the oxen, the donkeys, the camels and the garments (1 Samuel 27:9)".

In Samuel chapters 29-31, we have the story of Philistine warriors who gathered at Jezreel by the thousands to fight Saul. David with his men also went to Jezreel to join in the battle against their fellow countrymen. Their support, however, was viewed with suspicion and they were ordered to return to their village. When they returned to Ziklag, they discover that the Amalekites had burned their village and taken all their women, children, and animals.

David set out with his 600 men to rescue their families. During the arduous pursuit, he had to leave behind 200 exhausted men. With his smaller force of 400 men, David ambushed the Amalekite raiders and recovered all the women and children including his wives, Hinoam and Abigail. He also captured all the flocks and herds of the Amalekites. David magnanimously shared the spoils with his men, even the 200 exhausted men who had been left behind.

The author of 1 Chronicles 29:26-28 ended his text with this glowing tribute—"Thus David the son of Jesse reigned over all Israel. The time that he reigned over Israel was forty years. . . . Then he died at a good age, full of days, riches and honour."

Commentary

In 1 Samuel and 1 Chronicles, there is a smooth transition to power from Saul to David. David is courteous, respectful, and loyal to Saul making no attempt to seize the throne. There is no mention of Saul's son, Ishbosheth, being made king and an ensuing civil war that lasted over two years. David is fair and generous to his men. He is a spiritual leader who through prayer and sacrifices seeks to follow the will of God. He is humble. He can do no wrong.

There is no criticism of David who, while living under Philistine protection at Ziklag, offered to join the Philistine army against Saul. Nor is David condemned for his murderous attacks on the Geshurites, the Girzites, and the Amalakites. During these raids he and his men killed men, women and children and stole their property. It would appear that the injunctions of the Ten Commandments forbidding murder and theft only applied to the Hebrew tribes, and not to neighbouring tribes. Another more likely explanation is that many parts of the Torah (the Laws) were written long after the monarchy period.

David promised to build a temple for God in Jerusalem, but was forbidden to do so by God. "You shall not build a house for my name, for you are a warrior and have shed blood" (1 Samuel 28:2-3). Ironically God had sanctioned David's battles with the Philistines, the Moabites, the Edomites and the Syrians.

In 1 Samuel and 1 Chronicles the message is clear: David is a worthy successor to Saul—a model king, a great warrior and a holy man of God. It is not until we read 2 Samuel that we discover that David had a rival to the throne. We also discover a dark side to the character of David in several shocking anecdotes.

2 SAMUEL

In the first chapter we find different details about the death of Saul. Though mortally wounded, Saul pleaded with an Amalekite to end his suffering. The Amalekite slew Saul and brought his crown and royal amulet to David as proof that the king was really dead. Instead of rewarding the Amalekite, David ordered his immediate execution for slaying "the Lord's anointed".

David, after a period of grief at the loss of Saul and his son, Jonathon, then went to Hebron, thirty-two kilometers south of Jerusalem, where he was anointed as the king of Judah. Not everyone agreed with this coronation. Abner, commander of Saul's army, decided that Ishbosheth ought to be the rightful heir of Saul and made him the king of the northern tribes of Israel including the tribe of Benjamin. For the next two years there was bitter fighting between the forces of David and Ishbosheth. It ended with the assassinations of Abner and Ishbosheth. With their deaths, the elders of the northern tribes came to Hebron and pledged their allegiance to David.

Consolidated in power, David successfully campaigned against the Philistines, the Arameans, the Moabites and 20,000 Syrian foot soldiers. Other neighbouring states, recognizing the power of David, made peace with Israel and brought contributions of tribute to King David. After taking Jerusalem by force from the Jebusites (a Canaanite tribe that inhabited Jerusalem before the Jews entered Canaan), David made Jerusalem his new capital. Once David had settled in Jerusalem, he married more wives in addition to the six he already had, and acquired more concubines. In a great moment of celebration, David brought to Jerusalem the Ark of the Covenant—a gold-covered wooden chest holding the two stone tablets of the Ten Commandments.

Unlike 1 Samuel and 1 Chronicles, 2 Samuel included anecdotes that defamed the character of David, such as the infamous story of Bathsheba. (See chapters eleven and twelve). "It happened, late one afternoon, when David arose from his couch and was walking upon the roof of the king's house that he saw from the roof a woman bathing; and the woman was very beautiful." Her name was Bathsheba, the wife of Uriah, one of his commanders. David summoned her to his palace where he "took" her. When she became pregnant, David arranged for Uriah to die in battle. Bathsheba, oblivious of the circumstances of her husband's death, grieved for Uriah. After her period of mourning ended, David brought her to his house and she became his wife.

God showed his displeasure over David's conduct. "And the Lord afflicted the child that Uriah's wife bore to David, and he became sick"

(12:15). The child died. "Then David comforted his wife, Bathsheba, and went in to her and lay with her, and she bore a son, and he called his name Solomon (13:24).

There are more shocking anecdotes. Amnon, one of David's sons, raped his sister, Tamar, and then angrily rejected her. Homeless, she was taken in and cared for by her brother Absalom. We are told that David was angry, but there is no mention of David rebuking or punishing Amnon. Eventually, after two years, Absalom ordered his men to slay Amnon and then led a rebellion to overthrow his father.

In the ensuing conflict, Absalom took possession of one of David's homes where ten of David's concubines lived. Then Absalom "went in to his father's concubines in the sight of all Israel "(16:22). This is a euphemistic way of saying that Absalom raped his father's concubines. In the war that followed, Absalom's forces were defeated and Absalom killed. David was overcome with grief. "O my son Absalom, my son, my son Absalom! Would that I had died instead of you, O Absalom, my son, my son!" (18:33).

The scribes also mentioned a terrible famine that lasted three years. When David sought an explanation for this disaster, God blamed Saul. "There is bloodguilt on Saul and on his house, because he put the Gibeonites to death" (21:1). To make amends David turned over to the Gibeonites seven sons of Saul whom they subsequently hung at Gibeon.

The second book of Samuel concludes with a strange story of God ordering David to number the people of Israel and Judah. After the census was completed by Joab, the commander of the army, the Lord was so angry that he sent a "pestilence" that killed 70,000 men. To appease God David built an altar and offered burnt offerings and peace offerings. "So the Lord responded to the plea for the land, and the plague was averted from Israel" (24:25).

Commentary

David is given credit for bringing an end to a three-year famine by handing over the seven remaining sons of Saul to the Gibeonites. By doing so he brought closure to the Gibeonites who needed blood revenge for the murders Saul had committed against members of their tribe. I can't help but notice that by handing over Saul's sons, David rid himself of seven potential rivals to his throne.

In the last anecdote David ended a devastating plague by building an altar and offering sacrifices. It is a confusing story. God ordered David to take a survey of his people (only men were counted), but after the census was completed, God was so angry that he sent a plague that killed thousands of innocent people. It doesn't make any sense.

The scribe who wrote 1 Chronicles 21:1, had an answer. In this verse we learn that Satan persuaded David to count the people of Israel. God was not responsible. The plague was sent by Satan. It is not a satisfactory explanation, not only because it contradicts 2 Samuel, but also because it undermines the omnipotence and benevolence of a just God.

A more likely explanation is that people who lived in this pre-scientific era usually viewed natural disasters as punishments sent by the gods (or a god). Since the epidemic occurred right after the census, the author of 2 Samuel blamed the census-takers for the "pestilence".

✍ Author's Note

In Hebrew "Satan" means an accuser or adversary. In the O.T. there are only three references to Satan as found in Chronicles 2:1, the book of Job and Zechariah 3:1-2. The wily serpent of Genesis is portrayed more as a tempter than an adversary. The dualistic theology of a benefcent Creator opposed by a powerful "fallen angel" of darkness and evil evolved after the reign of Cyrus the Great of Persia due to the influence of Zoroastrianism. Thus, in the New Testament we find thirty-three references to Satan!

The scribe who penned the words, "O Absalom, my son, my son," tried to show a compassionate side to David, a leader who administered "justice and equity". The anecdotes, however, tell a different story—particularly the story of David lusting after Bathsheba and then deliberately planning the murder of her husband Uriah.

Then there is the story of Tamar, David's daughter, being raped by her brother. Although David was displeased, he did nothing! The saddest story for me is the one about his ten concubines who were raped by his son, Absolom. Did David express compassion for the humiliation and suffering of these women? Did he comfort them? In second Samuel 20:3 we learn the answer to these questions. "And David came to his house at Jerusalem. And the king took the ten concubines whom he had left to care for the house and put them in a house under guard and provided for them, but did not go into them. So they were shut up until the day of their death, living as if in widowhood".

Many people believe that King David wrote the Psalms, all one hundred and fifty of them. Most biblical scholars know that the psalms were compiled centuries after his death. Some of the psalms refer to events that happened in the sixth century, such as the Babylonian exile (See Psalm 137). It may well be that David was a skilled musician and lyricist who wrote some psalms. Maybe his name was mentioned as a heading to many psalms because he was a patron of the arts who supported musicians and poets. More likely, David was given credit for many of the psalms in order to enhance the importance of the psalms.

Solomon's reign began tumultuously because in the last days of his reign, David had not formally announced his successor. Adonijah, the fourth son of David, proclaimed himself king without consulting either his father or the prophet Nathan. As Adonijah and his guests celebrated his coronation, Bathsheba and the prophet Nathan anxiously spoke with David reminding him of his earlier promise that Bathsheba's son, Solomon, would be the next king. David immediately had Solomon anointed. "Then they blew the trumpet; and all the people said, 'Long live King Solomon!'" When Adonijah and his entourage heard the exaltations of the people, they fled in terror. Soon afterwards David died and Solomon ordered his commander, Benaiah, to kill Adonijah as well as Joab, an army commander who had supported Adonijah. Secure as king, Solomon ruled the united tribes of Israel and Judah for the next four decades.

In chapter four we find many examples of his wisdom, power, influence and wealth. When God appeared in a dream and asked Solomon what he would like to receive from his Lord, he asked only for wisdom and knowledge to govern his people. God, pleased with his humility, promised him unrivalled wisdom, wealth, and honour. These promises all came true. He was given credit for uttering 3,000 proverbs and for composing 1,005 songs. As well, the superscriptions of the books of Proverbs, Ecclesiastes and Song of Solomon all seem to give Solomon credit for their wisdom.

Solomon ruled over all the kingdoms from the Euphrates to the land of the Philistines to the border of Egypt; the countries under his control brought tribute and served Solomon all the days of his life. The tribute enabled Solomon to build 4,000 stalls of horses for his chariots. The tribute also helped Solomon to rebuild cities and construct many buildings using a forced levy of Israelites and thousands of slaves. Thus Solomon built a royal palace, a wall to enclose the city of Jerusalem, and, as ordered by his father David, a house of the Lord. Hiram, king of Tyre, supplied skilled workmen and building supplies in the twenty years that it took for these huge building projects. In return Solomon gave to Hiram twenty cities in the land of Galilee (1 Kings 9:10-14).

The Temple of Jerusalem was built with costly stones, cypress timber and cedars from Lebanon. The foundation stones were thirteen feet by sixteen feet. The main structure was one hundred feet long, thirty-three feet wide and fifty feet high. The inner sanctuary, containing the Ark of the Covenant, was thirty-three feet long, thirty-three feet wide and twenty feet high, overlaid with pure gold as was the altar. At the dedication of the Temple Solomon offered as peace offerings to the Lord, 22,000 oxen and 120,000 sheep.

His own royal palace house was also sumptuous in size and materials: 166 feet long, 83 feet wide and 50 feet high. Solomon would have needed such a home and more, for his 700 wives, princesses, and 300 concubines. The Queen of Sheba heard of the fame of Solomon and, after visiting him, gave him 120 talents of gold (9,000 pounds), spices and precious stones. "Thus King Solomon excelled all the kings of the earth in riches and in wisdom. And the whole earth sought the presence of Solomon to hear his wisdom" (1 Kings 10:23, 24).

King Solomon had many foreign wives, besides Pharaoh's daughter for whom he built a separate palace. Some of these foreign wives "turned away his heart after other gods" so that in his old age Solomon worshipped gods such as Ashtoreth, Milcom, and Chemosh. "And Solomon slept with his fathers and was buried in the city of David his father. And Rehoboam his son reigned in his place" (1 Kings 11:43).

Commentary

In reading the summaries of Solomon, you will have noticed a number of amazing "facts" that are best described by the word "grandiose". In 1 Kings you learned that Solomon had 700 wives, princesses and 300 concubines. At the dedication of the house of the Lord, 22,000 oxen and a 120,000 sheep were sacrificed to the Lord. When the Queen of Sheba visited Solomon she was so impressed that she gave him 9,000 pounds of gold. You don't have to be a cynic to conclude that these numbers are incredible exaggerations.

Although we are told in 1 Kings 10:23 that "King Solomon excelled all the kings of the earth in riches", he had to depend on a levy of forced, unpaid labour for his building projects. Lacking the cash to pay for the labour and supplies from King Hiram, Solomon had to concede twenty cities in Galilee as payment to Hiram.

Another hyperbole involves the size of Solomon's kingdom. In 2 Chronicles 9:26 we learn that Solomon's rule extended from the Euphrates, to the Philistines (Mediterranean), and even to the borders of Egypt. If that were the case, you would expect evidence of such a vast empire to have been mentioned in diplomatic correspondences with Egypt, Babylon or Assyria. That is not the case. In the annals of Assyria, Babylon, Persia or Greece, we find no evidence of Solomon's extensive empire, his magnificent buildings or his sumptuous wealth.

We are told in 2 Chronicles 8:1 that it took twenty years and thousands of labourers, craftsmen, and slaves to build Solomon's palace and the House of the Lord in Jerusalem. Archaeologists, however, have yet to discover remnants of these buildings even though the foundation stones of the Temple were reputed to have been sixteen by thirteen feet in size. Solomon had 4,000 stalls for his horses and chariots, but here, too, the physical evidence is missing.

For the past two hundred years, archaeologists have searched extensively for evidence to validate the O.T. accounts of the monarchy period. Following is an excerpt from the October 1991 edition of Ha'aretz Magazine. "Don't blink. This is what archaeologists have learned from their excavations in the land of Israel. . . . the united monarchy of David and Solomon, which is described in the bible as a regional power, was at most a small tribal kingdom". Dr. Israel Finkelstein,

Professor of Archaeology at Tel Aviv University, reached a similar conclusion in his book, "The Bible Unearthed" (2001). He described tenth century Jerusalem as a small town, built on a hill, with a modest palace and royal shrine.

Maxwell Miller Professor of Hebrew Bible and John Hayes Professor of Old Testament, co-authors of A History of Ancient Israel and Judah (1986), had this to say about Solomon. "Yet viewed in the broader context of the ancient Middle East, he is to be regarded more as a local ruler over an expanded city-state than as a world-class emperor. He engaged in the normal royal pursuits of his day—building programmes, commercial ventures, patronage of instructional and proverbial literature" (pg. 199).

After reading my commentaries and these last three quotations, I suspect that you may feel disillusioned because you assumed or were taught that the books of Samuel, Kings and Chronicles were historical records. As you can see in Addendum E, there are no external records or archaeological evidence, outside of the texts themselves, to validate the anecdotes and deeds of Saul, David and Solomon.

As noted in the Introduction, the scribes who compiled and redacted the texts of Samuel, Kings and Chronicles did so hundreds of years after the reigns of Saul, David and Solomon. Did time dull the memories of the scribes or did some numbers grow over the centuries as folk stories were retold countless times?

There is another explanation. The problem is that we have been conditioned to think of the books of the Old Testament as historical records rather than as literature with theological themes. If we focus on the incredulity of some of the stories, and the obvious exaggerations, we miss the theological points.

For example, a major theme in this monarchical period is that the Lord is not a passive observer. He is in control. He determines the destiny of all nations and particularly that of

Judah and Israel. If Yahweh wills it, then the Jewish armies will prevail or not. If the Jews must have a king, so be it, but Yahweh will choose their king even if he is a mere shepherd youth like David. If Saul is tormented by an evil spirit, it is a spirit sent by Yahweh. If David fights Goliath, it is the Lord who delivers him from the hand of the Philistine giant.

Another recurring theme is that the Hebrews must be faithful to Yahweh. They must worship only Him and not the gods of neighbouring tribes and nations. If they forsake Yahweh for other gods, they will face judgment and consequences. Saul sinned against Yahweh when he sought guidance and help from a medium who summoned up the spirit of Samuel from the realm of the dead. Saul died because of this "unfaithfulness". The great recurring tragedy is that the people, and particularly their kings, failed to worship only Yahweh and this apostasy led to judgment and terrible consequences.

Yahweh's promise to reward "faithfulness" is another important theme. In return for worshipping only Him, Yahweh promised David that his blood line would rule Israel forever. Yahweh's promise to the Israelites, in return for their faithfulness, was that they would possess the land of Canaan forever. Kings who were faithful to the Lord would die "at a good age, full of days, riches and honour" (1 Chronicles 29:28). Kings who were unfaithful died ignominiously without respect and honour (See 1 Samuel chapter 31 which describes the suicide of Saul).

These are some of the key theological themes that underlie the stories and anecdotes I have summarized. The books of Samuel, Kings and Chronicles make sense when we understand them as theological literature.

CHAPTER 10

The Breakup of Solomon's Empire

SOURCES: 1 KINGS AND 1 CHRONICLES,
2 KINGS AND 2 CHRONICLES

A FTER THE DEATH of Solomon in 925 BCE, his son Rehoboam was recognized as Solomon's heir by the Jews in the south (Judah), but not by those in the north (Israel). To unify his reign, Rehoboam travelled north to the city of Shechem to address the assembly of Israel. At this important meeting the northern officials promised to serve Rehoboam, but there were conditions. "Your father made our yoke heavy. Now therefore lighten the hard service of your father and his heavy yoke on us, and we will serve you" (1 Kings 12:4).

Rehoboam refused to compromise. Instead, he promised even heavier burdens. He said, "Whereas my father laid on you a heavy yoke, I will add to your yoke. My father disciplined you with whips, but I will discipline you with scorpions" (1 Kings 12:11). To enforce his dictates, he appointed Adoram, a taskmaster who had experience in supervising forced labour. These decisions were not well received. The Israelites stoned Adoram to death and Rehoboam fled in his chariot back to the safety of Jerusalem.

The tribes in the north had another leader in mind—Jeroboam. Previously he had been an overseer for Solomon in charge of the forced labour needed to construct the royal buildings. Although we don't know exactly what he did, we know he "lifted up his hand against the king" and then had to flee to Egypt where he was given a safe refuge by the

Pharaoh Shishak. After the death of Solomon, Jeroboam returned to Israel to attend the meeting at Shechem. Soon afterwards he was chosen to be the king of Israel.

With the collapse of the reconciliation talks at Shechem, Judah and Israel existed side-by-side as two, separate kingdoms. It was not an amicable separation. As reported in 1 Kings 14:30, "There was war between Rehoboam and Jeroboam continually."

"In the fifth year of King Rehoboam (c.919 BCE), Shishak, king of Egypt, came up against Jerusalem. He took away the treasures of the house of the Lord and the treasures of the king's house. He took away everything (1 Kings 14:25-26)." According to the scribes of Kings and Chronicles, Yahweh orchestrated this invasion to punish Judah because they had forsaken the laws of the Lord, and Rehoboam had angered the Lord by building shrines in the high places to foreign gods, and by allowing male cult prostitutes to practice their "abominations".

The Kingdom of Israel, under king Jeroboam, was guilty of the same offenses. The prophet Ahijah made dire predictions to the wife of the king. He prophesied that another king would soon rule over Israel, that Jeroboam and his heirs would die, and that the Lord would smite Israel as a reed is shaken in the water.

Commentary

Although the author of 1 Kings 14:30 thought that there was a continuous war between Rehoboam and Jeroboam, we have no physical evidence or written records of major battles. It is likely that the "war", which lasted for four decades, consisted of border skirmishes in the buffer zone of the territory of the tribe of Benjamin. The settlements in the north were strong and numerous—a formidable area for the Judeans to subdue.

Shishak's campaign was real. His conquest of both Israel and Judah is described on an inscription on one of the walls of the Theban temple of Amon. From the cities listed, historians can tell that this military campaign was waged mainly in the north against Israel. It seems likely that when Shishak's army reached Judah, Rehoboam made peace with the invaders by giving tribute money to save Jerusalem. He capitulated without resistance; whereas in the north, cities were plundered and razed.

The author/compiler of 1 Kings frequently criticized Judah and Israel for paying homage to other gods such as Baal. Both kingdoms were also condemned for making numerous Asherims—a cult object related to the worship of the fertility goddess Asherah. As a result of this idolatry, Yahweh, angry and jealous, sent the Pharaoh Shishak to invade Canaan and to take away the treasures in the Royal Palace and the Temple of Jerusalem. This interpretation of events reiterates two familiar themes—Yahweh controls the destinies of the nations, and national disasters happen when Yahweh's people do what is evil in the sight of their Lord.

We have already noted in the texts we have examined thus far that idolatry was a common practice in Judah and Israel. In the tenth and ninth centuries BCE, it is likely that many Jews saw nothing wrong in worshipping more than one god. Looking back at those centuries, what we find is polytheism, not monotheism. The concept of ONLY one god came later—by the prophets Amos, Hosea, Micah and Isaiah in the eighth and seventh centuries BCE.

CHAPTER 11

The Demise of the Northern Kingdom of Israel

ISRAEL, WHICH SEPARATED from Judah in 925 BCE, existed as a separate kingdom until 722 BCE. As the scribes of Chronicles and Kings looked back (more than a century later) at the calamitous events that had befallen Israel, they wanted their readers to understand why the northern kingdom had collapsed. Why had Yahweh allowed a foreign power to take control of part of Canaan, their promised land? Why had Israel suffered such a crushing defeat? Why were many Israelites scattered throughout the Assyrian empire? As we now cover the reigns of kings, such as Ahab of Israel and Ahaz of Judah, we will see the answers of the scribes to these questions.

AHAB (873-851 BCE)

Ahab reigned over Israel from the capital city of Samaria for twenty-two years and "did more to provoke the Lord, the God of Israel, to anger than all the kings of Israel who were before him" (1 Kings 16:33). One of his many provocations was his decision to marry Jezebel, a non-Jew. Ahab also built an altar to her god, Baal, in the capital city of Samaria, and made an Ashram (a cult object of the fertility goddess Asherah).

This idolatrous behaviour did not go unnoticed. Elijah, a prophet in Israel, condemned Ahab for worshipping the Canaanite gods and prophesied that the Lord would punish Ahab by a terrible drought. Some who heard these proclamations were furious, including King Ahab and Queen Jezebel. Fearing for his life, Elijah fled into the wilderness where he miraculously survived thanks to ravens that brought him bread and meat. A widow also helped Elijah to survive the famine by giving him the last of her dwindling supply of food. After Elijah prayed for her, Yahweh rewarded her with a jar of meal that fed her family for weeks and a jug of oil that was never empty. When the woman's son became ill and died, Elijah prayed to the Lord, "and the soul of the child came into him again and he revived."

To end the drought the Lord ordered Elijah to confront Ahab. The encounter turned into a contest between the prophet of Yahweh and the prophets of Baal and Ashram. Elijah challenged these 850 prophets to call upon their gods to light a fire for the sacrifice of a bull. They prayed earnestly, but to no avail. After dousing the sacrificial animal with water, not once, but three times, Elijah called upon Yahweh and fire fell from the heavens and consumed the bull. Then Elijah said to those who had witnessed this miracle, "Seize the prophets of Baal; let not one of them escape" (I Kings 18:40). As a final proof of Yahweh's power, Elijah prayed for rain and the heavens grew black with clouds and wind, and there was a great rain. The drought was over.

When Ahab returned to Samaria and told Jezebel what had happened, Jezebel vowed to find and kill Elijah. Not surprisingly, Elijah fled again into the wilderness with no provisions. This time he was saved by an angel who gave him a jar of water and a cake baked on hot stones. This meal sustained him for the next forty days and nights as he journeyed to Horeb (known in Judah as Sinai), the mount of God. There he witnessed a great wind, an earthquake, and a fire. Finally he heard a whisper. It was the voice of the Lord telling him to anoint Hazael as king over Syria, Jehu as king over Israel, and Elisha as his successor. (I Kings 19)

On the last day of his earthly life, Elijah, in the company of Elisha, rolled up his mantle and struck the waters of the Jordan River. The water parted and the two prophets walked to the other side on dry ground. As they walked and talked the two men were separated by a chariot of fire and horses of fire, and Elijah was taken up into heaven in a whirlwind.

Thus the Prophet Elisha succeeded Elijah as a spokesman for Yahweh and he, too, was a miracle-maker. He used the mantle of Elijah to part the waters of the Jordan river; he found miraculous streams of water in the wilderness of Edom to sustain the armies of Judah and Israel in their war with the king of Moab; he cured Naaman, the Syrian commander, of leprosy; he foretold the defeat of the Syrian army; he multiplied barley loaves; he provided a widow with an unlimited supply of oil in her jar; he enabled a barren wife to have a child; he, also, raised a son from the dead (2 Kings 4, 5).

Commentary

It should come as no surprise to us that the scribes judged Ahab as one of the worst kings of Israel, and that they made no mention of Ahab's successes as a ruler. During Ahab's reign trade and commerce flourished particularly in the cities of Israel. He received no praise for his military accomplishments. Ahab was part of an alliance of kings that stopped an Assyrian invasion led by Shalmaneser III. Together they halted the enemy army at the battle of Qarqar in 853 BCE. (We know this from Assyrian records—the Monolith Inscription and the Black Obelisk. (See Addendum E.) To the scribes, however, he was still an evil, idolatrous leader.

Nor should we be surprised that the scribes depicted Jezebel, the wife of Ahab, as an idolater and murderess. She is portrayed as the one responsible for the building of the shrine to Baal, and the murder of Yahweh's prophets (1 Kings 18:13). She was also a temptress. Due to Jezebel's lies and encouragement, Ahab confiscated the vineyard of their hapless neighbour, Naboth.

In blaming Jezebel for all these crimes, the scribes of Kings and Chronicles were following a familiar pattern of portraying women as temptresses and traitors. Solomon, too, in his last years was led astray by his foreign-born wives to worship their gods. Samson was betrayed by his Philistine wife, Delilah. The daughters of Lot slept with him after they made him drunk with wine. And then there was Eve! The story of Jezebel is another example of the post-exilic scribes using the power of the quill to blame women for the actions of men.

The miracles of Elijah and Elisha are unbelievable if interpreted literally, but they do make sense when viewed as allegorical stories intended to show these prophets as powerful instruments of God. According to the scribes, both prophets parted the waters of the Jordan River just as Moses parted the waters of the Red Sea. Elijah and Elisha were depicted purposefully in the tradition of Moses.

In these miracle stories we find another subtle message. The Jews in the southern kingdom revered Jerusalem as the focal location for the worship of Yahweh. The Temple of Jerusalem was the Lord's temple where sins were forgiven, people were healed, and prayers were answered. The Temple was the link between man and God, earth and heaven. This was the ideology of the scribes who compiled the books of Kings and Chronicles. This partisan perspective, however, is not what we find in the stories of Elijah and Elisha. Here were two prophets who heard and conveyed the Word of Yahweh in Israel (not in Judah). Their prayers for rain to end a terrible drought were answered. They raised the dead. All these deeds were accomplished many miles distant from the city of Jerusalem and the House of the Lord.

From the numerous references to other gods, the scribes were reminding their readers that during the reigns of kings, such as Ahab, Yahweh was in competition with the Canaanite gods of Baal and Asherah. Jezebel and Ahab were not the only ones guilty of idolatry; many others in Israel also paid homage to gods other than, or in addition to, Yahweh. This competition between Yahweh and the Canaanite gods could well have been rife with violence as we see in the story of Elijah ordering the execution of 850 prophets of Baal and Asheram. Keeping in mind that the scribes wrote this story many years after the reign of Ahab, we should take the number killed with a large grain of salt.

KING AHAZ (ALSO KNOWN AS JEHOAHAZ I) (KING OF JUDAH FROM 732-715 BCE)

During King Ahaz's reign, the Assyrian kings struggled to hold their empire together. Rezin, the Syrian king of Damascus and Pekah, the king of Israel, advocated rebellion. When Ahaz refused to join this dangerous venture, Rezin and Pekah joined forces and marched on Jerusalem. Even when Ahaz saw their combined forces just outside the walls of Jerusalem, he refused to join their coalition. In this decision, he was supported and encouraged by the prophet Isaiah.

Once the siege began, Ahaz was filled with fear and doubt. To reassure Ahaz, the Lord offered a sign as proof that Jerusalem would survive and his enemies would perish.

"Behold, the virgin shall conceive and bear a son, and shall call his name Immanuel. He shall eat curds and honey ... For before the boy knows how to refuse the evil and choose the good, the land whose two kings you dread will be deserted. . . . The Lord will bring upon you and upon your people ... the king of Assyria. (Isaiah 7:14-17)

Commentary

These verses of Isaiah 7:14-17 have been the source of much controversy. The authors of the gospels of Matthew and Luke viewed these verses as a prophetic foretelling of the birth of Christ. Most biblical scholars question this interpretation for a number of reasons. In the Hebrew text of Isaiah 7:14 the scribes used the word "Alma" which means a young woman of marriageable age, and not the Hebrew word for virgin, which is "betulah". When the book of Isaiah was translated into Greek, the translators used the Greek word "parthenos" which meant "virgin". This was an unfortunate and misleading misinterpretation, one that was used by those who compiled the King James Version of the Bible, and one that was also used in the version of the Bible I am using here. (The ESV® Bible)

To interpret Isaiah 7:14 as a prophetic foretelling of the birth of Jesus, we have to ignore the context; namely, hostile forces had encircled Jerusalem because Ahaz had refused to rebel against Assyria. If the siege had succeeded, Jerusalem would have been sacked, and Ahaz and his family either killed or taken as slaves. The name of the unborn child was a message meant to alleviate the fears of Ahaz. "Immanuel" means "God is with us". Isaiah was trying to assure Ahaz that Jerusalem would not fall to the army outside their walls. Isaiah also predicted in 7:16 that Jerusalem would be saved and the enemies of Ahaz would perish <u>before</u> the yet unborn child could mature enough to know the difference between evil and good. That is what happened.

The siege failed. In 732 BCE the Assyrian army under Tiglath-pileser III defeated the Syrian forces, destroyed their capital, Damascus, and executed Rezin. Then he installed Hoshea as a puppet king of Israel. Thus Israel received a temporary reprieve and was allowed to exist as a vassal state of Assyria.

Amos, a prophet of Judah, travelled north to Israel to deliver scathing warnings and prophecies. At Bethel, home to the royal sanctuary, he chastised Israel not only for their worship of pagan deities and their rejection of the laws of the Lord, but also for trampling the poor. He cited these words from God, "I hate, I despise your feasts, and I take no delight in your solemn assemblies … But let justice roll down like waters, and righteousness like an ever flowing stream" (5:21-24). His prophecies were also ominous. He predicted domination and punishment by a foreign power, deportation and exile for Israel, and a violent death for Jeroboam the king of Israel.

These prophecies were not well received. Amaziah, the high priest of Bethel, denounced Amos for these frightful prophecies and banished him from ever again preaching in Israel. Forbidden to return to Israel, Amos returned to Jerusalem where he made sure his voice would be heard by writing the Book of Amos. "The Lord roars from Zion, and utters his voice from Jerusalem" (1:2). His warnings were in vain.

HOSEA

Hosea, a prophet of Israel, also prophesied prior to the fall of Israel in 722 BCE. He told his audience that he had been told by the Lord to marry a prostitute and to have her children. It was a clever, metaphorical warning. Hosea represented the people of Israel and the prostitute represented the foreigners who had been brought in by the Assyrians and who had become the wives of Israelites. "Upon her children I will have no mercy, because they are children of whoredom".

His message was bleak and dark, similar to that of Amos. "There is no faithfulness or steadfast love, and no knowledge of God in the land: there is swearing, lying, murder, stealing, and committing adultery; they break all bounds and bloodshed follows bloodshed" (4:1-2). In addition to giving birth to "alien" children, the people of Israel had forgotten the true meaning of worship.

"For I desire steadfast love and not sacrifice, the knowledge of God rather than burnt offerings" (6:6).

The warnings of the prophets Amos and Hosea went unheeded. Hoshea, the last king of the Kingdom of Israel, invoked the ire of Shalmaneser V, king of Assyria, by approaching Egypt as an ally and by withholding the yearly tribute. Consequently, "In the ninth year of Hoshea, the king of Assyria captured Samaria and he carried the Israelites away to Assyria and placed them in Halah, and on the Habor, the river of Gozan, and in the cities of the Medes. And this occurred because the people of Israel had sinned against the Lord their God" (2 Kings 17: 6, 7). With this final defeat and deportation, the kingdom of Israel ceased to exist. To replenish the depleted Jewish population, the Assyrians brought in thousands of subjects from parts of other conquered areas to live in Israel.

Commentary

In the nine chapters that comprise the Book of Amos, it is important to note that Amos never acknowledged the existence of any deity except Yahweh, whom he respectfully praised as the creator of the earth (4:13) and the cosmos (5:8). In Amos we find monotheism.

After the disastrous defeat of Israel in 722 BCE, the deportation of thousands of Israelites, and the resettlement of other exiled people to Israel, it was inevitable that some of the newcomers intermarried with the Jews of Israel. This was viewed by the Judean scribes and priests who returned from the exile as an abomination. They looked with disdain at the Jews who still lived in Israel, as well as the imported foreigners who had brought with them their own gods and religious traditions. Even when some of the foreigners accepted

Yahweh and the Torah, the Judean scribes and priests viewed them with contempt.

Jesus was aware of this scornful prejudice and racism when he told the parable of the Good Samaritan, centuries later. Jesus purposefully made a Samaritan the hero, the one who helped a man who had been beaten and robbed and left half dead by the roadside. After he told the parable, Jesus asked a lawyer which person had proved himself to be a good neighbour—the priest who passed by on the other side, the Levite who did likewise, or the Samaritan who stopped to help. When the lawyer answered, he could not bring himself to say "the Samaritan" (one from the former capital of Israel). Instead he replied, "The one who showed mercy on him" (Luke 10:29-37).

In summary it is fair to say that 722 BCE was a disastrous year in the annals of Hebrew history. It marked the end of the northern Kingdom of Israel. Yet, as the authors of Kings, Chronicles, Isaiah, Amos and Hosea reflected on this tragic period in their history, they saw the hand of Yahweh in all that had transpired. It was Yahweh who brought a message of hope to Ahaz during the siege of Jerusalem. It was Yahweh who then sent the Assyrians to defeat Rezin and Pekah. It was Yahweh who sent the Assyrians to defeat and to deport many Israelites.

Their explanation was theological, not political. "And this was so because the people of Israel had sinned against the Lord their God" (2 Kings 17).

CHAPTER 12

The Demise of the Southern Kingdom of Judah

(722 BCE to 586 BCE)

~~~~~~~~~~~

I N 722 BCE the northern kingdom of Israel lost its status as a nation. Judah avoided a similar fate by remaining a vassal state of Assyria and by making regular payments of tribute. Thus the small landlocked nation of Judah still existed, but as a pawn in the hands of the powerful nations of Assyria, Egypt, Babylon, and Persia.

From 722 BCE to 586 BCE there were many kings of Judah as noted in 2 Kings, 2 Chronicles, Jeremiah and the Book of Isaiah. While the scribes judged many of these kings as evil, they much admired two kings, Hezekiah and Josiah. It was a perilous time to reign because the political landscape kept changing—sometimes with disastrous results as we shall see.

KING HEZEKIAH (REIGNED FROM 715-686 BCE)

Hezekiah was considered one of the "good" kings. He repaired and cleansed the Temple; he offered sacrifices to atone for the sins of all of Israel; he destroyed the "high places" and the altars of the Canaanite goddess, Asherah; he reinstituted tithing to support the Temple and the priests, and he revived the tradition of the Passover to commemorate the Exodus from Egypt. According to the scribes, "He did what was good in the eyes of the Lord".

Politically he made two costly decisions. One, he formed a dangerous and worthless alliance with Egypt (Isaiah 30, 31). Two, ignoring his advisers, he stopped making tributary payments to Assyria. As a result, in 701 Sennacherib, king of Assyria, arrived with an army. After subduing forty-six walled cities of Judah, he began a siege of Jerusalem. Hezekiah and the prophet Isaiah beseeched Yahweh to intercede. "And that night the angel of the Lord went out and struck down 185,000 in the camp of the Assyrians" (2 Kings 19:35). Sennacherib returned to Nineveh where his own sons murdered him as he worshipped in the temple of his god, Nisroch. For the time being, Hezekiah and Judah were safe.

Commentary

At the siege of Jerusalem, Yahweh sent "an angel" of death to the camp of the Assyrians. Although some interpret this incident literally, the most likely explanation is that the siege ended because many soldiers were ill or died of cholera or dysentery. In the eyes of the scribes, however, it would still have been "an angel of the Lord" that slew the Assyrian soldiers.

After the death of Sennacherib, the Assyrian Empire faced many challenges. The vast empire established by Tiglath-pileser III, Shalmaneses V, and Sargon II was clearly in a period of decline. It took King Ashurbanipal (669 to 630 BCE) four years to quell a civil revolt. During his reign he also had to deal with the growing menace in the north of the Cimmerians, the Scythians and the Medes. In the south he had to contend with the military and political threat of Egypt whose Pharaohs pressured vassal states like Judah to break free from Assyria.

The city state of Babylon, however, posed the greatest danger. In 612 BCE King Nabopolassar of Babylon (aided by the Medes, Scythians and Cimmerians), besieged, sacked and depopulated Nineveh, the Assyrian capital. In 605 BCE at the battle of Carchemish, Nebuchadnezzar defeated the combined force of an Egyptian army and the last remnants of the Assyrian army. With this victory, the Neo-Babylonians (also referred to as the Chaldeans) became the new Middle Eastern power. Keeping in mind these historical events, we turn now to the reigns of the last four kings of Judah—Josiah, Jehoiakim, Jeconiah and Zedekiah.

KING JOSIAH OF JUDAH (639-609 BCE)

The scribes judged Josiah as an ideal ruler. He repaired the temple and ensured that all the workmen were paid for their services; he followed the laws of Yahweh and cleansed the temple of all false idols and cult prostitutes; he tore down the shrines in the high places and got rid of the mediums and wizards; he reinstituted the keeping of the Passover (2 Kings 22).

Although Josiah turned to the Lord "with all his heart and soul" and brought about sweeping religious reforms, "still the Lord did not turn from the burning of his great wrath, by which his anger was kindled against Judah" (2 Kings 23:26). His great wrath is explained in 2 Kings 22. Judah (and this included even King Josiah) had to pay the penalty for forsaking the laws of Moses and for practising idolatry. Thus Josiah, who had been promised a peaceful demise in 2 Kings 22:20, met an untimely and violent death when he went out to meet the Pharaoh of Egypt at Megiddo. More disasters followed for the kingdom of Judah.

KING JEHOIAKIM (REIGNED 609 TO 597 BCE)
KING JECONIAH (R. 3 MONTHS IN 597 BCE)

In 609 BCE Jehoiakim (the grandson of Josiah) was appointed king of Judah by Necho II, king of Egypt. Judah had now become a vassal state of the Egyptians. After the battle of Carchemish, Nebuchadnezzar marched unopposed into Syria-Palestine and conquered the Philistine city of Ashkelon. Then he returned to Judah to punish and subdue the king and his subjects. He besieged Jerusalem. To avoid its destruction and his own demise, Jehoiakim paid tribute and handed over some of the royal family as hostages. Judah became a vassal state of the Babylonians.

In 601 Jehoiakim switched his allegiance back to Egypt and withheld tribute payments to the Babylonians. The results were catastrophic. In 597 BCE Nebuchadnezzar arrived with an army and again besieged Jerusalem. According to the book of Jeremiah, Jehoiakim died during the siege and his body was cast outside the city walls (Jeremiah 22:19). After a twelve-month siege, Nebuchadnezzar captured and looted the city, and carried away whatever treasures remained in the Temple and Royal Palace.

To further punish Judah and to minimize future rebellions, "He carried away all Jerusalem and all the officials and all the mighty men of valour, 10,000 captives, and all the craftsmen and the smiths. None remained, except the poorest people of the land" (2 Kings 24:14). Their recently appointed king, Jeconiah (son of Jehoiakim) was exiled as a prisoner to Babylon.

KING ZEDEKIAH (REIGNED FROM 597 TO 586 BCE)

Nebuchadnezzar appointed Zedekiah, a "king to his liking", but he too did "what was evil in the sight of the Lord". He made an alliance with Egypt and, counting on Egyptian support, rebelled against the king of Babylon. Nebuchadnezzar returned with his army and laid siege to Jerusalem for two years. When the food supplies were exhausted,

Zedekiah and his men tried to escape by breaching the wall. Their escape was thwarted, their army scattered and their king captured.

Nebuchadnezzar showed no mercy. "They slaughtered the sons of Zedekiah before his eyes, and put out the eyes of Zedekiah and bound him in chains, and took him to Babylon" (2 Kings 25:7). The Babylonian army again razed and plundered the city but this time they also destroyed Solomon's Temple. Many leaders were executed, and the elite of their society were taken as captives to Babylon. Only the poorest of the citizens were left with their economy shattered.

The southern kingdom of Judah was finished, but the Jewish narrative was far from over.

CYRUS THE GREAT (R.559 TO 530 BCE)

From the Iranian Plateau a new leader emerged, one who would build the largest empire yet seen in this part of the world. In 539 BCE, Cyrus the Great, after defeating the armies of the Medes and Lydians, invaded Babylon and the Neo-Babylonian Empire became part of the Persian Empire. Once again the political landscape had changed, but this time for the benefit of Judah.

Cyrus was a statesman who respected the customs and religions of the countries he had conquered. After defeating the Babylonians, one of his first acts was to issue a general declaration that had profound implications for the Jews. This declaration, known as the Cyrus Cylinder (See Addendum E), was discovered in 1879 in the ruins of a Babylonian temple. The text extols Cyrus as a great benefactor chosen by the god Marduk to restore peace and order. Although there is no mention of Jews, Jerusalem or Judea, the declaration called for the repatriation of displaced peoples and the restoration of their cults and temples of worship. Consequently some of the exiled Jews living in Babylon returned to their homeland and helped to rebuild the Temple of Jerusalem. Most importantly, the scribes and priests who returned began to compile the epic narrative of their nation that we have been studying since the first chapter in this book.

Commentary

The scribes of the O.T. who described these events saw the hand of the Lord in all that had transpired. It was the Lord who gave Cyrus the kingdoms he conquered. It was the Lord who stirred up the spirit of Cyrus to make his famous declaration. It was the Lord who inspired Cyrus to help build and pay for a new temple for Jerusalem (as detailed in the Book of Ezra). Isaiah referred to Cyrus as a shepherd of the Lord and as "his anointed"—the only non-Jew to be given this messianic title in the Old Testament (Isaiah 45:1).

With Persia now holding the reins of power throughout the Middle East, there must have been a collective sigh of relief from the exiled Jews living in Babylon, as well as their countrymen living in Jerusalem and the rest of Judah. The Jews in Babylon could now return to their homeland and help to rebuild the temple that Nebuchadnezzar had razed to the ground. Nevertheless there was still a sense of uncertainty for this tiny, traumatized nation that had endured centuries of strife and suffering from the Edomites, the Moabites, the Ammonites, the Philistines, the Egyptians, the Assyrians and the Babylonians. What now lay in store for them under the new Persian Empire? What would happen to them in the future? These concerns are addressed in the next chapter— the answers of the Prophets.

✍ Author's Note

The fall of Israel and Judah also provides the setting for many other O.T. books. This context sheds light on the books of Lamentations, Habakkuk, Ezekiel, Daniel, Nahum, and Jonah. With your indulgence, I will briefly summarize these books to show the impact of the demise of the Jewish kingdoms of Israel and Judah.

The Book of Lamentations: In these five chapters the "weeping prophet" Jeremiah bitterly grieves the plight and suffering of Israel and

Judah. During his lifetime, he saw terrible disasters: the devastation inflicted by Nebuchadnezzar's army, the deportation of thousands of Judeans to Babylon, and the destruction of the Temple of Jerusalem. With much pain he reiterates the familiar explanation for what has befallen his countrymen. "Woe to us, for we have sinned!"

The Book of Habakkuk: The prophet laments the brutality of the Babylonians while at the same time justifying the violence. It happened because Judah had sinned. Even though he was perplexed by the terrible events that had happened, he still taught that "the righteous shall live by faith" (2:4).

The Book of Ezekiel records seven visions of the prophet Ezekiel while he was in exile in Babylon. There are three themes—judgments against Israel, judgments against the nations, and future blessings for Israel.

The Book of Daniel: This book refers frequently to the kings of Babylon and Persia. In a number of verses there are references to monsters and angels. It is a difficult book to read not only because of its symbolism, but also because it combines secret revelations with visions of "the end of times". In the next chapter I will examine more closely this intriguing book.

The Book of Nahum: In this short book Nahum gloats over the fall of Nineveh. "The Lord is avenging and wrathful; the Lord takes vengeance on his adversaries" (1:2). We can understand the tone of this book when we remember that the author lived through years of Assyrian oppression until 612 BCE when the Babylonians defeated the Assyrians and sacked their capital city of Nineveh.

The Book of Jonah (commonly known as "Jonah and the Whale"). This text is sometimes ridiculed as a puerile fable. It is not. When you read this story in its context of Near Eastern History, I think you will feel empathy for the writer as he tried to make sense of the tragedies that had befallen his country.

You are familiar with the story line. The prophet Jonah was summoned by Yahweh to go to the capital city of a country he hated. "Arise, go to Nineveh, that great city, and call out against it, for their evil has come up before me" (1:2). Instead of obeying the Lord, Jonah fled to the coastal port of Jaffa and from there boarded a ship bound for Tarshish. Soon after they set sail, there was a great storm. Jonah, oblivious to the raging sea, slept soundly in the hold of the ship. The terrified crew decided that Jonah was to blame and threw him into the sea. At once the waters were calm. Then a great fish (the text does not say "whale") swallowed him. While in the belly of the fish (three days and three nights), he prayed to the Lord and vowed to be loyal. "And the Lord spoke to the fish, and it vomited out Jonah upon the dry land" (2:10).

Jonah immediately went to Nineveh and prophesied that in forty days the city would be overthrown. The king and citizens, alarmed at the words of this "man of God", repented of their evil ways. God then changed his mind and decided not to send a foreign invader to capture and plunder Nineveh.

Jonah was shocked and angry that Yahweh was willing to act graciously and mercifully. Jonah wished he were dead. Yahweh tried to console him with these words: "Should not I pity Nineveh, that great city, in which there are more than 120,000 persons who do not know their right hand from their left, and also much cattle?" (4:11). It is an abrupt ending to the story and we are left wondering if Jonah followed the example of Yahweh and tempered his hatred of Nineveh with some degree of mercy. It is a strange ending, but one that makes senses when we consider the story in its historical context.

Commentary

The Assyrians had a standing army of professional soldiers. With their armour, their chariots, their archers and engineers skilled at breaching the defences of fortified cities, the Assyrians had the most formidable armies yet seen in the Middle East. If a city refused to surrender, it was ravaged. In Assyrian inscriptions, their kings frequently boasted of destroying, devastating and burning cities that had resisted. Sometimes conquered officials were flayed to death and their bodies impaled at the gates of their cities as a warning to others. To discourage future resistance, the Assyrian kings deported thousands of captives throughout the empire. (Source: Babylonian Chronicles)

The scribe who wrote the story of Jonah knew all this. He also knew what the Assyrians had done to King Zedekiah, and his sons. What he could not understand was why Yahweh had permitted these atrocities and the deportation of thousands of his fellow Judeans to Babylon. Why did He not smite them?

The scribe posed a possible answer. Perhaps Yahweh permitted them to live in peace and prosperity because He was merciful. Perhaps Yahweh gave them time to repent of their evil ways and to seek His forgiveness. Thus, the scribe wrote this intriguing story of the prophet Jonah fleeing from his mission to preach to the citizens of Nineveh. Yahweh thwarted his flight by a raging sea and a great fish that swallowed him, only to spit him up on the shore when Jonah decided to obey his summons.

It is a powerful allegory and when we read the story as such, we get the message and understand the anguish of the scribe as he struggled to reconcile his faith in Yahweh with the harsh realities of Assyrian rule and domination.

CHAPTER 13

The Prophets

~~~~~~~~~~~~

W HO WERE THE prophets? If you are Jewish you might say that
they were spokesmen for God who called on their fellow Jews
to worship only Yahweh, to follow the Torah, and to show mercy and
kindness to the weak and poor. They also predicted the end of times
and the coming of a Messiah from the line of David. If you are from
a Christian background, you might add that the prophets foretold the
ministry of Jesus, the Messiah. If you are an evangelical Christian you
might emphasize what the prophets preached about the "last days"—a
time of tribulation, war, divine judgment, and retribution.

ISAIAH (740 – 680 BCE)

*The vision of Isaiah the son of Amoz, which he saw concerning Judah and
Jerusalem in the days of Uzziah, Jotham, Ahaz, and Hezekiah, kings of
Judah (Isaiah 1:1).*

These four Jewish kings reigned during the Assyrian era of domination. In this time-frame the northern Kingdom of Israel was destroyed,
thousands of its citizens deported throughout the Assyrian Empire,
and the depopulated areas resettled by non-Jews from other conquered
territories. The southern Kingdom of Judah escaped these disasters by

becoming a vassal state of Assyria. These traumatic events form the setting for the Book of Isaiah.

In Isaiah 45:1 we have an additional, later context that links the Book of Isaiah to the Persian Empire. *Thus says the Lord to his anointed, to Cyrus, whose right hand I have grasped, to subdue nations before him and to loose the belts of kings.* Since Cyrus is mentioned it is evident that the Book of Isaiah covered at least one hundred and sixty-five years of rule by the Assyrians, the Babylonians and the Persians. Obviously Isaiah's ministry did not extend to this entire period. Thus, biblical scholars have concluded that the book of Isaiah was written, compiled and edited by more than one author over many decades.

In chapter one Isaiah detailed the terrible events that occurred under Assyrian domination. He saw these disasters as Yahweh's punishment for Israel's and Judah's immorality and infidelity. Though angry and dismayed by the past iniquities of his people, Isaiah did not reject his people. He looked to the future with hope envisaging a Jewish nation redeemed by righteousness and justice.

In Isaiah 2:3-4 we find an uplifting prophecy of universal peace and brotherhood, a time without poverty, crime or war. In that day nations would look to Zion (Jerusalem) for spiritual and moral guidance, and Yahweh would be the great arbitrator, not only for the Jews, but for all nations. Wars would cease and men would be farmers not warriors. *For out of Zion shall go forth the law, and the word of the Lord from Jerusalem. He shall judge between the nations, and shall decide disputes for many peoples; and they shall beat their swords into plowshares, and their spears into pruning-hooks; nation shall not lift up sword against nation, neither shall they learn war anymore".*

This would happen because God would send a Messiah, one anointed from the lineage of King David, to bring justice and righteousness for Israel and all the nations. *"There shall come forth a shoot from the stump of Jesse . . . and the Spirit of the Lord shall rest upon him . . . with righteousness he shall judge the poor, and decide with equity for the meek of the earth . . . and with the breath of his lips he shall kill the wicked . . . The wolf shall dwell with the lamb, and the leopard shall lie down with the young goat ... for the earth shall be full of the knowledge of the Lord as the waters cover the sea"* (11:1-9).

The Messiah would be more than a righteous judge. He would lead them against the Moabites, Egyptians, Philistines and the Babylonians. All their enemies would feel the wrath of the Lord, and be defeated and humiliated. Under their Messiah's command, *they shall swoop down on the shoulder of the Philistines in the west, and together they shall plunder the people of the east. They shall put out their hand against Edom and Moab, and the Ammonites shall obey them. And the Lord will utterly destroy the tongue of the Sea of Egypt* (11:14, 15).

With their enemies defeated, Jews who had been scattered abroad would return to Judah. *In that day the Lord will extend his hand yet a second time to recover the remnant that remains of his people, from Assyria, from Egypt ... and from the coastlands of the sea"* (11:11).

Commentary

The Messiah that Isaiah envisaged was both a spiritual leader and a warrior. Like King David, he would rule justly and righteously, and lead them in battle to triumph over their enemies, and vindicate the Jews as the chosen people of God.

Before we examine the book of Jeremiah, I would like to consider three controversial verses from Isaiah 53:3-5. **"He was despised and rejected by men; a man of sorrows, and acquainted with grief; Surely he has borne our griefs and carried our sorrows; yet we esteemed him stricken, smitten by God, and afflicted. But he was pierced for our transgressions, he was crushed for our iniquities."**

To whom does the "he" refer? To answer this question we need to examine the context—the chapters that preceded these verses. In chapter 41:8 we read, "But you, Israel, my servant . . ." In chapter 49:3 we find, "You are my servant, Israel, in whom I will be glorified". In chapter 52:13 we read, "Behold my servant shall act wisely; he shall be high and lifted up". When viewed in the context of these verses, I think it is clear that the suffering servant is a metaphorical reference to the Jewish nation—a servant who was bruised, crushed and humiliated by Yahweh as punishment for many transgressions.

Unfortunately, Christians usually interpret these verses as a prophetic reference to the suffering and death of Jesus, as Handel did when he composed The Messiah. I have no issue with pastors, priests and theologians who see a parallel here to the life and ministry of Jesus, but to interpret these verses from Isaiah 53 as a direct reference to Jesus is to ignore the context of the previous chapters: a context that depicts Israel as the suffering servant.

JEREMIAH (593-585 BCE: THE YEARS OF HIS MINISTRY)

Born into a priestly family, Jeremiah was painfully aware of the oppression and suffering of his people under the Assyrian conquerors and then the Babylonians. With anguish he exhorted King Zedekiah and the people to repent of their sins of idolatry, injustice and immorality. He exhorted the king and priests not to turn to the Egyptians as an ally, but to accept the yoke of the Babylonians. For delivering these sermons of repentance, doom and submission, Jeremiah was reviled, beaten, and imprisoned. He almost died in prison.

Nonetheless, Jeremiah saw hope for his countrymen, as did Isaiah. *Behold, the days are coming, declares the Lord, when I will raise up for David a righteous Branch, and he shall reign as king and deal wisely, and shall execute justice and righteousness in the land. In his days Judah will be saved, and Israel will dwell securely* (Jeremiah 23:5). Jeremiah also had a message of reassurance for the Jews who had been scattered abroad by the Assyrians and Babylonians. *I will bring them back to their fold, and they shall be fruitful and multiply* (23:3).

Commentary

Jeremiah witnessed Nebuchadnezzar's invasion and pillage of Jerusalem, the destruction of the temple in 587 BCE, and the deportation of thousands of his countrymen to the city of Babylon. These events explain the somber tone of the Book of Jeremiah, sometimes called "the weeping prophet". He is also thought to have been the author of Lamentations. In both books we see a despondent author, but one who did see light at the end of a long black tunnel in his prophecies of the Messiah and the return of those carried abroad by their conquerors.

EZEKIEL (C.622-570 BCE)

If you read the first three chapters as prose, you may be confused. Read them as poetry, however, and they make sense. In these introductory chapters, Ezekiel painted a vivid picture of Yahweh as a powerful wind with lightning and thunder—a warrior riding on his battle chariot surrounded by heavenly creatures. *Such was the appearance of the likeness of the glory of the Lord. And when I saw it, I fell upon my face, and I heard the voice of one speaking* (Ezekiel 1:28). Thus, with poetic drama Ezekiel introduced himself as one called by God to be a prophet and a watchman over Israel.

In succeeding chapters Ezekiel gave a detailed explanation for the woes and persecution of his countrymen; namely, Yahweh had judged and punished them for their idolatry and failure to practice social justice. One of his favourite metaphors was to compare Judah to a wife-prostitute. His dire prophecies were fulfilled. In 587/86 BCE Ezekiel witnessed the brutal occupation of Jerusalem and the demolition of the temple by the forces of Nebuchadnezzar. Along with thousands of other captives, he was exiled to Babylon.

Not all of his prophecies were doom and gloom. In the latter chapters, Ezekiel foresaw many future blessings for his nation. He saw a day when all the exiled Jews would return to their homeland, and Israel and Judah would once again be one nation under a Davidic king. The temple would be rebuilt and Yahweh would return to reside there. These messages of hope are epitomized in Chapter 37:1-14 by the vision of a valley full of dry bones. Ezekiel is ordered by God to bring all the dry bones to life. Ezekiel does as he is commanded and a great host stood upon their feet—alive again.

Commentary

"Them bones, them bones, them dry bones. Hear the word of the Lord". By these memorable words, Ezekiel offered assurance and hope to his countrymen in Judah, as well as those in captivity. Through the analogy of dry bones coming to life, Ezekiel prophesied that the kingdoms of Israel and Judah, would one day be revived and reunited.

Although Ezekiel was a strong advocate for worship and ritual, he also insisted on justice and righteousness for the poor and oppressed. In chapter 18, he spelled out in great detail his vision for social justice—one that was similar to what we have seen in Isaiah and Jeremiah. He foresaw a time of judgment, wrath and punishment for Judah and for the nations that had humiliated Israel and Judah. He saw a day when all Jews would return from captivity and be part of one nation under a messianic king of the line of David. He prophesied that the temple would be beautifully and fully restored (chapters 40-48).

Concluding Comments on the Prophets

I see Isaiah, Jeremiah and Ezekiel as courageous, spiritual leaders who dared to criticize kings and high priests, and to hold them accountable for their words and deeds. Appalled at the plight of widows and orphans, the prophets were outspoken advocates for the powerless and poor in their society.

I have not included the twelve Minor Prophets: Hosea, Joel, Amos, Obadiah, Jonah, Micah, Nahum, Habakkuk, Zephaniah, Haggai, Zechariah, and Malachi. When you read these books, you will find that many of their pronouncements and prophecies are similar to the three prophets we have examined.

You may also wonder why I did not include Daniel alongside the prophets we have just examined. This may come as a surprise to you, but the religious leaders who determined the cannon of the Hebrew Bible placed the book of Daniel under "the writings", not under "the prophets". Jewish scholars contend that the Book of Daniel was written at least four centuries after the Books of Isaiah, Jeremiah and Ezekiel. From the following summary of the book of Daniel, you can see the basis for this conclusion.

DANIEL

Most readers assume that the book that bears the name "Daniel" was written in the sixth century because of the many references to Babylonian and Persian kings. That is what I thought when I studied the O.T. at Emmanuel College in the 1950's. Most theologians today think otherwise because in the Book of Daniel we find references to four historical periods: the Babylonian Empire (605-539 BCE), the Persian Empire (539-323 BCE), the thirteen years of conquest by Alexander the Great (336-323 BCE) and, after the subsequent division of his empire, a Hellenistic state ruled by Seleucid kings from 323-63 BCE. Consequently, many scholars contend that the Book of Daniel was written and compiled c.165 BCE during the reign of the Seleucid king, Antiochus IV Epiphanes.

Antiochus IV added the title "Epiphanes" to his name. The term means "God manifest"—a title he bestowed on himself and had imprinted on his coins. Others, who knew how he had dealt with the Jews, preferred to call him a "madman". His cruel treatment of the Jews was recorded by Josephus in *War of the Jews* and by the authors of the Books of the Maccabees, the leaders of the Jewish rebellion against the Seleucid dynasty.

What Antiochus did was appalling. In order to impose Greek culture on the Judean population, he replaced the High Priest of Jerusalem with one who was sympathetic to the Greeks. He confiscated funds from the Temple treasury and for a price appointed Menelaus to become the next High Priest. During Menelaus' tenure some of the sacred temple vessels were stolen. The pious Jewish population was enraged at these events. There were riots and two civil rebellions that were violently crushed by Antiochus. After the second rebellion, Antiochus outlawed Judaism and banned circumcision, the study of the Torah, and the keeping of Jewish dietary laws. As a final sacrilege, he placed a statue of Zeus in the Temple and sacrificed swine on the altar!

Failure to follow the harsh edicts of Antiochus became a matter of life and death for Jews who were determined to be faithful to their beliefs and traditions. Such were the times for the unknown author of the Book of Daniel. To inspire and embolden his fellow Jews to observe their Jewish laws and to worship only Yahweh, he wrote stories about a legendary, heroic figure from the past known as Daniel, whom he depicted as an educated and handsome Jewish noble who was exiled to the king's palace in Babylon along with three of his friends. By pretending to be writing about Babylonian despots of the past, the author cleverly conveyed his message to his countrymen without incurring the wrath of the Seleucids. I will recount three stories with which you are likely familiar.

In chapter two Daniel interpreted a dream that greatly disturbed Nebuchadnezzar, a dream that none of the Babylonian seers could explain. Without even being told the contents of the dream, Daniel described the dream to the amazement of the king (2:31-35).

This image, mighty and of exceeding brightness, stood before you, and its appearance was frightening. The head of this image was of fine gold, its chest and arms of silver, its middle and thighs of bronze, its legs of iron, its feet partly of iron and partly of clay. As you looked, a stone was cut out by no human hand, and it struck the image on its feet of iron and clay, and broke them in pieces . . . but the stone that struck the image became a great mountain and filled the whole earth.

Daniel explained that the "mighty" image represented five kingdoms. The head represented Nebuchadnezzar, king of the Babylonians. The breast and arms represented the kingdom that would follow. The belly and thighs represented a third kingdom which would rule over all the earth. The legs and feet represented a fourth divided kingdom. The stone, not made by humans that shattered the legs, was Yahweh who would establish a fifth kingdom on earth that would never be destroyed.

The author, writing from the vantage point of 165 BCE, was referring metaphorically to the rise and fall of the Babylonians, the Persians, Alexander the Great, and the subsequent division of the Greek empire. These earthly kingdoms had come and gone, but when Yahweh would establish his kingdom on earth, it would last forever. It was a message of hope and reassurance.

The second story is well-known. Three friends of Daniel (Shadrach, Meshach, and Abednego) were thrown into a fiery furnace because they refused to bow down and worship the golden idol that Nebuchadnezzar had set up. When the king looked into the furnace, he was amazed to see a fourth figure in the midst of the fire. It was an angel. The three men walked out of the furnace and not a hair of their heads had been singed. The "golden idol" was a metaphor, a reference to the statue of Zeus that Antiochus brought into the Temple of Jerusalem and ordered the Jews to worship!

In chapter six we have the story of Daniel thrown into a den of lions because he prayed to Yahweh and not to the king. For his faithfulness, the Lord intervened and Daniel was unharmed by the lions. This story was also meant to inspire. Just as the Lord saved Daniel from the lion's den, so the Lord would save faithful Jews who had the courage to disobey their oppressor—Antiochus.

Commentary

Although Babylonian kings are the villains in these three stories, there is no evidence from the books of Nehemiah, Isaiah and Ezekiel that they were intolerant of Judaism. Under the Babylonians the Jews in Judah and in captivity were free to worship Yahweh and to follow their religious traditions. The synagogue had its origin in Babylon!

The editors of the Jewish Encyclopaedia have dated the Book of Daniel to the time of Jewish persecution during the reign of the Syrian king Antiochus Epiphanes. That is also the conclusion of the biblical academics listed at the end of this chapter. These scholars interpret the "beasts", described in chapter seven, as metaphorical allusions to Babylon, Persia, Alexander the Great and the Seleucids. They see the "little horn" in chapter eight as a reference to Antiochus IV—the "madman" who tried to stamp out Judaism.

Many of the Jews who suffered under the tyranny of Antiochus must have welcomed the apocalyptic book of Daniel about the "end of times". Here was a message to counter their sense of defeat and despair, because Yahweh would soon intervene. He would punish the wicked through a Messiah of the lineage of David, one who would defeat their enemies and usher in a new order of peace.

Many Jews, emboldened by the stories of Daniel and the apocalyptic prophecies of Isaiah and Ezekiel, strongly resented being subjected to Greek culture, and rebelled against the Seleucids. The Maccabees, a Jewish rebel army, took control of Judea and ruled from 164-63 BCE. This successful revolt put successive generations of rebels in a dangerous frame of mind, one that led to three disastrous wars with Rome.

After the first Great Revolt of 63-73 BCE, the Romans destroyed most of Jerusalem, and the second temple. Many Jewish leaders were killed, exiled or taken to Rome as slaves. The Qumran community (where the Dead Sea Scrolls were found) was razed to the ground and at Masada, the last stronghold of the rebels, 960 defenders committed mass suicide as a final act of defiance. The last Bar Kokhba's Revolt occurred from 132-136 CE with dire consequences: the Judean population was almost wiped out, Judaism was banned, Jews were forbidden to live in Jerusalem and the province of Judea was renamed as Syria Palestina. With this final blow the Jews lost their status as a nation!

SCHOLARS WHO DATE DANIEL TO C.165 BCE

1. Professor C.L. Seow of Vanderbilt University (2003, p.1-2) *Daniel.*
2. Professor Sibley L. Towner of Union Presbyterian Seminary (1984, p.34-36) *Daniel.*
3. Professor Paul R. Redditt of Georgetown College (2008, p.187) *Introduction to the Prophets.*
4. Professor John L. Collins of Yale University (1984, p. 87) *Daniel: With an Introduction to Apocalyptic Literature.*
5. Professors Matthews and Moyer of Missouri State University (2012) *the Old Testament: Text and Context.*
6. Professor Diane L Jacobsen of Union Theological Seminary (1991) *A Beginner's Guide to the Books of the Bible.*
7. Professor John Dominic Crossan of DePaul University (1991, p. 239) *the Historical Jesus.*
8. Editors of the Encyclopaedia Britannica.

CONCLUSION

~~~~~~~~~~~~~~~

WE HAVE COME to the end of the Old Testament narrative. We
began our study with the creation of the cosmos, followed
by stories of Adam and Eve, and Noah and the Great Flood. Then
we moved to 1900 BCE as a small family led by Abraham set out for
Canaan from the city-state of Ur, located at the mouth of the Euphrates
River on the Persian Gulf. Thus began many centuries of a nomadic
existence—the era of the Patriarchs. It ended when the Hebrews fled
to Egypt due to drought and famine. There they survived as slaves for
300 years. Their bondage came to an end with the epic tale of Moses
who led the Hebrew slaves out of Egypt to the Sinai desert where they
wandered for forty years. After the Hebrew tribes settled in Canaan,
Judges governed the scattered tribes. This period was followed by one of
unification under the monarchs. We focused on the "golden age" of Saul,
David and Solomon. After the subsequent breakup of the united Jewish
Kingdom, we covered the devastating demise of the Kingdom of Israel
by the Assyrians, and the subsequent subjugation of the Kingdom of
Judah by the Babylonians, Persians and Seleucids. Lastly we considered
what the prophets wrote: their explanations for these tragic events, their
call for social justice, and their prophecies of the future.

As I traced this narrative from Adam to Daniel, I did so in its context
of Near Eastern History—a setting crucial to our understanding of
many events and stories in the Old Testament (such as the story of
Jonah and the great fish).

With a few exceptions, such as the Book of Daniel, the scribes and priests wove together this narrative in the post-exilic period of the sixth century BCE. They had specific objectives. They wanted to give their disillusioned citizens an official history—one that would explain the catastrophes they had suffered at the hands of their enemies, one that would reaffirm their faith in Yahweh, and one that would inspire their countrymen to follow their laws and traditions. Knowing when and why the scribes compiled and edited these ancient texts also helped us to make sense of the narrative.

As we looked back at this "official" history, we did so from our vantage point in the twenty-first century. With our knowledge of science, history and literature, we knew that parts of the narrative were problematic and could not be interpreted literally, particularly the accounts of creation, the first man and woman, and the Flood. Thus in Addendum C, we analytically examined the story of Noah and the Ark. When interpreted literally, we saw how the story defied both science and reason. In Addendum A we examined the geological clocks that scientists used to date the earth as 4.5 billion years old. Our DNA, outlined in Addendum B, gave us a different perspective from the story recounted by the scribes of Adam and Eve. There was no instant creation a few thousand years ago. According to molecular genetics, our species, Homo sapiens, came out of Africa about sixty thousand years ago! In Addendum D I included a Sumerian code of law that was written centuries before the Ten Commandments because people tend to think of the Ten Commandments as our earliest moral code. Lastly, in Addendum E I listed some of the archaeological evidence that relates to the O.T.

Some of you may have been surprised to learn that the scribes, in recounting their earliest beginnings, "borrowed" extensively from Mesopotamian folklore. I pointed out earlier, similar stories from the Sumerians who recorded their stories of creation on clay tablets that are carbon dated to c.1600 BCE (See "Enki and Ninhursag: A Paradise Myth"). Sumerians also had a Flood story dated c.2500 BCE ("The Epic of Gilgamesh" Tablet X). There were precedents also for the Ten Commandments from Egypt ("Papyrus of Ani" Addendum D), from

Sumeria (Addendum D: the Code of Ur-Nammu) and from Babylon (Code of Hammurabi c.1760 BCE). The Hebrew scribes of the sixth century BCE would have been familiar with such folklore, but there were no laws prohibiting plagiarism. Copyright laws did not exist until after the invention of the printing press.

The most problematic part of the narrative for me was that of Moses and the Exodus. From my Sunday school lessons to lectures at Emmanuel College, I was taught that Moses was a real person, one of the founders of Judaism, a spiritual leader from whom we received the Ten Commandments. Decades later I was shocked when I read *Did Moses Exist—the Myth of the Israelite Lawgiver* by D.M. Murdock, written in 2014. The gist of her book is that the Exodus never happened. She claimed there was no external evidence that Moses ever existed or that he led thousands of Hebrews through the Sinai desert to a land of milk and honey.

Was Murdock correct? In chapter four I reviewed the research of academics on whether or not the Exodus occurred. The most convincing analysis was that of Dr. Israel Finkelstein, a Professor at Israel's Tel Aviv University. He is well-known as a leading scholar of the archaeology of the Middle East, and the author of the best seller, *The Bible Unearthed: Archaeology's New Visions of Ancient Israel and the Origin of its Sacred Texts* (2001). His research confirmed the thesis of D.M. Murdock that the story of Moses and the Exodus was indeed folklore.

Folklore does not mean it is nonsense. It means you have to look for the reasons the story was written and for the meanings behind the story. That is what I did in my concluding commentary of the Exodus in chapter four. This brings us to the crux of making sense of the O.T.

Although it is important to know the historical context, as well as the reasons why the scribes compiled their narrative, the Old Testament is not so much about history as it is about theology. Consider for example the book of Job—a masterpiece of prose and poetry. Alfred Tennyson called it "the greatest poem of ancient and modern times". After you have read the summary and my commentary, you may agree with Tennyson, or perhaps not.

The main character is Job, a "blameless and upright man, who fears God and turns away from evil" (1:8). Satan, however, questions Job's motives contending that Job is a "good" man for selfish reasons. Satan contends that Job is a righteous man because he believes that the good will be blessed with prosperity and the evil will be punished. God disagrees with Satan's assessment and allows Satan to test Job. Consequently, all of Job's herds of oxen, sheep and camels are slain, along with almost all of his servants. Then a powerful storm brings down his house killing his seven sons and three daughters. Although wracked with grief, Job does not curse God. Instead he says, "Naked I came from my mother's womb, and naked shall I return. The Lord gave, and the Lord has taken away; blessed be the name of the Lord" (1:21).

Satan is still not convinced of Job's integrity because Job did not suffer any physical pain. "All that a man has he will give for his life. But stretch out your hand and touch his bone and his flesh, and he will curse you to your face" (2:5). So God permits Satan to afflict Job with "loathsome sores" from the sole of his foot to the crown of his head. Even then Job does not curse God, although he curses his birth. With exquisite poetry, he rues the day he was born (3:1-26).

Three of Job's friends visit him trying to make sense of what has befallen their friend. They raise questions that have long troubled mankind. Why do bad things happen to good people? Why do the righteous suffer? How do you vindicate God as being just in the light of human suffering? The friends cite traditional answers which Job rejects. He is adamant that he has done nothing to deserve his losses and pain. He questions the justice of God.

Finally God appears out of a whirlwind, but instead of answering these important questions about the suffering of good people and divine justice, God admonishes Job for assuming that he, a mere mortal, could understand His mind and purpose in creating the vast cosmos. Job repents. He apologizes for questioning and doubting God.

There is a happy ending to the story. The Lord forgives Job and blesses him with twice the number of herds that he once owned. He fathers ten more children and lives to be a great-great-grandfather. He dies at the age of 140.

Commentary

Here is folklore that resonates with theology. It is a story that reiterates a theme that we have encountered many times in the narrative; namely, Yahweh controls the destiny of nations and individuals.

It was Yahweh who orchestrated the end of the Kingdom of Israel by sending in the Assyrians to conquer them and scatter their citizens abroad. It was Yahweh who used Nebuchadnezzar to defeat the Assyrians and to bring the Judeans under Babylonian rule. It was Yahweh who sent the Persian king, Cyrus, to defeat the Babylonians and to pass an edict that freed the Hebrews who had been exiled to Babylon.

Sometimes, however, His ways are inscrutable, as in the Book of Job which raises the vexing question of why the righteous suffer. When the story ends the question remains unanswered. God speaks to Job out of the whirlwind, but He doesn't explain why the righteous sometimes suffer.

This ending is in stark contrast to the prophets who taught that people suffer as punishment for their sins. In Job we find a different perspective. Sometimes the righteous suffer horribly, as in this story of a good man who lost his property, his children, his servants and his health. Job dismissed the argument that Yahweh was testing him as trite and insulting. In the end Job found no alternative but to trust in God. It is a powerful statement of faith that has brought comfort to many in times of tragedy and loss.

***

Today, however, many people find it difficult to take this step of faith. In my lifetime there have been numerous tragedies that have caused unimaginable suffering and loss to innocent children and adults— insidious diseases and viruses; the civilian "collateral" damage from wars fought in Europe, the Middle East, Africa and Asia; the Holocaust; the killing fields of Cambodia; Hurricane Katrina and world-wide acts of terrorism.

How do you reconcile these events with faith in a benevolent Creator of love, wisdom and purpose? Who is in charge of the cosmos and our own little planet, Earth?

Thank you for your investment of time and effort in reading my summaries and critiquing my commentaries and addenda. In this journey together, we have noted and examined many tenets of faith in the context of Near Eastern history. I hope making sense of the Old Testament has motivated you to examine your own faith and to arrive at your own conclusions.

EPILOGUE

~~~~~~~~~~~~~~

Although we have completed our study of the OT narrative, the Jewish narrative continues to unfold to this day. It is an amazing story of resilience and survival, but it is also a heart-breaking story of "man's inhumanity to man". The Diaspora, which began with the dispersion of Jews from their homeland by the Assyrians and the Babylonians, was perpetuated brutally by the Romans in the first and second centuries of the Christian era. Emperor Hadrian expelled and resettled hundreds of thousands of Jews from Judea throughout the Middle East and Europe.

Dispersed with no ruler, and no political or military clout, the Jews banded together in their scattered communities determined to maintain their faith, their identity and their traditions. While they succeeded in fulfilling these noble aspirations, their future was bleak for ahead of them loomed centuries of prejudice, humiliation and persecution.

The Broadway musical *Fiddler on the Roof* gave us a glimpse of what life was like for Jews in Imperial Russia in 1905. This production was based on a book by Shalom Aleichem, titled *Tevye the Milkman*. It depicted the repressive living conditions that Jews endured under the Tsars. Life was so harsh that from 1881 to 1914 almost two million Jews emigrated from Russia to the United States.

Although the Koran advocates tolerance towards the Jews, "the People of the Book", Muhammad expelled two Jewish tribes from Medina and slaughtered the male adults and male children of a third tribe. Jews living in Arab countries were known as *dhimmis* and as such had to pay a special tax (jizya). They were not allowed to bear arms or to give testimony in most Muslim court cases. In Persia, Jews were forced to convert to Islam during the sixteenth and seventeenth centuries. In Yemen during the seventeenth century Jews were given the choice of becoming Muslims or living in a remote desert area (the Mawza Exile). The Jewish Virtual Library lists many more inequities and atrocities that the Jews experienced under Islam.

Jews living in European countries fared even worse because many Christians held Jews to be responsible for the crucifixion of Christ, and labeled their Jewish neighbours "Christ-killers". This charge often incited mobs to attack Jews and their communities. It wasn't until March 2, 2011 that Pope Benedict XVI unequivocally declared that the Jews were not responsible for the death of Jesus. It came too late for the Jews in the German cities of Speyer, Worms, and Mainz when their communities were violently attacked and looted in 1096 during the First Crusade. It came too late for the Jews who were expelled from England after King Edward I issued an Edict of Expulsion in 1290. It came too late for the Jews in Spain who in 1492 were given the choice of becoming Catholics or leaving the country. It came too late for the Jews in Italian cities who were forced to live in walled ghettoes by the infamous decrees of Pope Paul IV in 1555 (*Cum nimis absurdum*).

Adolf Hitler capitalized on the anti-Semitic rhetoric of his day by blaming the Jews for Germany's defeat in W.W.I and for their post-war economic woes. In his book *Mein Kampf*, he expounded his theory of Aryan supremacy and classified Jews as the most inferior of the races. Emboldened by Hitler, countries like Iraq, Libya, Egypt, Syria and Yemen made life so harsh for their Jewish residents during the 1940's, that there was a mass exodus of c.900,000 Jews from these Arab countries. This exodus was nothing compared to what happened next—the deportation of millions of European Jews to concentration camps and the extermination of 6,000,000 men, women and children.

After World War II, some Jews were repatriated and returned to their pre-war countries, but many did not because there was nothing left to which to return, or because it was unsafe and dangerous to do so.

Consequently, in 1945 and 1946 close to two million Jews languished in refugee camps in Germany, Austria and Italy. Countries like France and Britain, struggling to rebuild their countries and economies, set strict quotas on Jewish refugees. So did countries with land and resources such as the United States and Canada! To resolve this humanitarian and political crisis, in 1948 the United Nations created the State of Israel. It was a pragmatic, political decision that was vehemently opposed by many Arab nations.

***

In this epilogue I have briefly summarized an incredible story of survival by a resilient and courageous race of people who have endured centuries of prejudice, persecution, dispersion and genocide. I conclude with a quotation by Anne Frank who died on July 15, 1944, three months short of her sixteenth birthday, while imprisoned at Bergen-Belsen, Germany.

"It's a wonder I haven't abandoned all my ideals, they seem so absurd and impractical. Yet I cling to them because I still believe, in spite of everything, that people are truly good at heart. It's utterly impossible for me to build my life on a foundation of chaos, suffering and death. I see the world being slowly transformed into a wilderness. I hear the approaching thunder that, one day, will destroy us too. I feel the suffering of millions. And yet, when I look up at the sky, I somehow feel that everything will change for the better, that this cruelty too shall end, that peace and tranquility will return once more. In the meantime, I must hold onto my ideals. Perhaps the day will come when I'll be able to realize them!"

(pg. 332 *The Diary of a Young Girl*, Doubleday Publishers, 1995.)

ADDENDUM A

Geological Clocks

~~~~~~~~~~~~~~

You MAY WONDER why many people in North America believe that the cosmos was created 6,000 years ago. I do have an explanation—one that goes back to Archbishop James Ussher of Ireland who lived from 1581-1656. To determine the exact date of creation, he added up all the generations outlined in the Bible from Adam to Jesus, and concluded that God began his first day of creating in 4004 BCE. If you then add the subsequent years, you can see how Ussher determined that our cosmos was created around 5,650 years ago. His chronology was an honourable, rational timeline for his generation. He had no knowledge of the following three "geological clocks" that you studied at high school, college or university.

1 – FOSSILS AND SEDIMENTARY ROCKS

Aeons ago, dead plants and life forms were sometimes buried in sediments such as mud, limestone, sand or volcanic ash. The softer parts rotted but the harder more durable parts remained. With the passage of time the sediment surrounding them hardened into sedimentary rocks, due to the pressure of subsequent layers of sediment and the weight of water. Thus, the outlines of some of these life forms were preserved. We call these outlines fossils, petrified remains of long-dead organisms.

According to geologists and biologists, when we go back millions and millions of years, we discover that life forms were less complicated—simpler. This is what we find in the fossil records. The earliest fossils are those of bacterial cells (single-celled organisms), and later, more complex forms of multi-cellular life forms. When we study vertebrate fossils, we see that fish came first, then reptiles, then birds, and lastly, mammals.

"THE MAP THAT CHANGED THE WORLD" BY WILLIAM SMITH

William Smith (1769–1839) is renowned today as the founding father of English geology. As a surveyor he had an important role in the building of canals throughout England—canals that carried goods such as coal. As these canals were dug, he took careful notice of the different layers of rock and the fossils in the rocks. Over his lifetime, he made meticulous notes and diagrams of sedimentary layers and fossils. He made several logical conclusions. One, if rocks from different sites contain the same fossils, they were from the same era. Two, if some fossils found in lower strata were not found in higher strata, they had become extinct.

To share these important discoveries, he painstakingly drew a beautiful, hand-painted map of what lay beneath the surface of England and Wales. Eight feet high and six feet wide, it was, indeed, a scientific breakthrough. To examine his research, I recommend Simon Winchester's *The Map that Changed the World*, published in 2001 in New York by Harper Collins.

Smith's map and notes had profound implications for geology and religion. For example, Smith observed that the oldest fossils found at the lowest strata of sedimentary rock (Pre-Cambrian—earlier than 545 million years ago) contained single-celled marine organisms. The organisms in the Cambrian era (545–495 million years ago) were more complex and multi-celled. In other words organisms had become more complex with time. These observations directly contradicted the widely-held belief in Smith's day that life was created in six days, 6,000 years ago.

Using fossils as relative indicators of time, geologists have subdivided the strata into three large-scale blocks of time. The Paleozoic Period (550 to 250 million years ago) contains the skeletons of petrified life forms. The Mesozoic Period (186 to 66 million years ago) contains the skeletons of different petrified organisms. In other words another major extinction of species had occurred. This era ended with the extinction of dinosaurs. We are currently in the third geological era, the Cenozoic Period.

From our knowledge of these underlying strata of our planet, we know the earth is indeed old. It takes time to turn sand, limestone, volcanic ash or mud into solid rock. How can a scientist determine that one layer of rock is c.2 billion years old or that the earth is c.4.55 billion years old? These questions bring us to the second geological clock—radioactive decay.

2 – RADIOACTIVE DECAY

To understand this geological clock I consulted a brilliant, gregarious high-school teacher of science—my brother Bill. Following are the notes I made that help me to understand the science of geological dating.

- All matter (every solid, liquid, gas and plasma) is composed of substances we call elements. There are over 100 (118 and counting) unique substances such as gold, carbon, helium and hydrogen. These substances cannot be separated into simpler substances.
- Each element is made from tiny identical particles called atoms. Every atom is composed of a nucleus, one or more protons, and usually a similar number of neutrons.
- The number of protons in the nuclei defines the element to which the atom belongs. For example a platinum atom has 78 protons, but add one more proton and it becomes gold.
- Some of the elements found in rocks and magna (brought to the surface of the Earth by earthquakes and volcanic action) are unstable; their nuclei (protons and neutrons) break down spontaneously

into smaller nuclei, releasing energy in the process. This process is known as radioactive decay.

+ Uranium 238 is an example of an unstable element because the nuclei of their atoms are continually releasing energy. Two types of particles are emitted. Alpha decay involves emissions of helium nuclei (two protons and two neutrons) and Beta decay involves emission of an electron. The discharge of these particles is the cause of the "clicks" in a Geiger counter.

+ As uranium 238 decays, it changes into different elements—such as protactinium 234, thorium 230, radium 226, radon 222, astatine 218, polonium 214, bismuth 210, polonium 210, and then with a final alpha decay to lead 206. Uranium undergoes decay at a constant and measurable rate. Thus, the ratio of Lead 206 to Uranium 238 in a rock sample gives an accurate measure of the age of the rock. The half–life value of Uranium 238 to become Lead 206 is 4.5 billion years.

+ Scientists use a mass spectrometer to measure the ratio of uranium to lead. This method of dating was developed at the University of Chicago by Clair Cameron Patterson. From 1948–1953, he collected rock samples from around the globe. By using a mass spectrograph to measure the ratio of uranium to lead isotopes, he determined that the earth was 4.55 billion years old (plus or minus seventy million years). His work has stood the test of time. His estimate of the age of the earth is still accepted in 2018.

3 – CARBON 14

Carbon 14 is another radioactive element used by scientists to determine the age of substances such as trees and bones. Carbon 14 forms when cosmic rays collide with nitrogen atoms in the earth's atmosphere. Some of these radioactive carbon atoms are absorbed into living organisms such as trees. When a tree dies it no longer absorbs Carbon 14 atoms;

subsequently, its Carbon 14 begins to undergo radioactive decay at a measurable rate with a half-life of 5,730 years.

Using this knowledge, scientists can take a piece of wood from an ancient tomb, and compare its reading of Carbon 14 with the amount of Carbon 14 from a living tree. The ratio provides an accurate measure of the age of the wood in the tomb. Or to simplify the explanation, if carbon from a piece of wood in an ancient burial site contains only half as much Carbon 14 as Carbon 14 from a living tree, the age of the old wood is approximately 5,730 years.

This method of dating gives a good fix on the age of organic matter, but only up to a point. After eight half-lives, only 1/256 of the original radioactive carbon remains, which is too little for a reliable measurement. This means that this method of carbon-dating is only accurate for objects up to forty thousand years old.

Scientists, however, have a much better method of Carbon 14 dating—mass spectrometry or atomic spectrometry. By this process only a few grams or milligrams of a sample are ionized, accelerated and passed through a magnetic field. Using this process scientists can date samples of wood or bone that are 70,000 years old.

***

How old is the Universe? Astronomers now consider the universe to be 13.7 billion years old. To understand how they arrived at this age, you may research the following web sites: Cepheid variable stars, the Hubble Site, WMAP (Wilkinson Microwave Anisotropy Probe) and NASA.

Molecular Genetics

~~~~~~~~~~~~

YOU MAY ALREADY know that DNA has a lot to say about the migratory history of man. It is truly amazing to realize that in our DNA we see the genetic footprints, not only of our parents and grandparents, but also those of earlier ancestors who lived hundreds of generations ago.

Human DNA (deoxyribonucleic acid) was first identified as a distinct molecule by Friedrich Miescher in 1869. Thanks to the contributions of Rosalind Franklin, Maurice Wilkins, James Watson, and Francis Crick, we know that these molecules exist in the form of a three-dimensional double helix. It resembles a spiral staircase.

DNA is a long, linear sequence of small molecules called nucleotides. There are four nucleotides that make up the linear sequences—cytosine (C), guanine (G), adenosine (A), and thymine (T). These are the "building blocks of life". In essence DNA is a genetic blueprint that encodes all the genetic information needed for each species to grow, function, and reproduce.

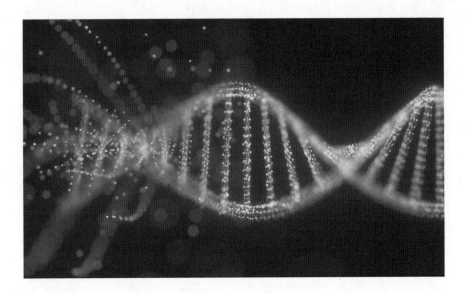

In the nucleus of each human cell there are forty-six chromosomes (twenty-three chromosomes from the sperm of the father and twenty-three chromosomes from the egg of the mother). In 1991 the scientists at the Sanger Centre in Cambridge England unraveled the DNA of a single human chromosome, number twenty-two. In deciphering this chromosome, they identified 679 genes; a gene is a short segment of DNA that codes for a specific trait. By June of 2000 all of the chromosomes had been decoded!

The term genome is used to refer to the twenty-three pairs of chromosomes. The human genome contains about 23,000 genes. All humans on earth are 99.9% genetically identical! The innumerable ways in which we can differ from one another are encoded in the remaining 0.1% of the genome.

We also differ because as cells divide (a constant process of growth and development in infants, children, and young adults, and of replacement and repair in adults), there are occasional mutations which may be considered copying errors. If a mutation is passed on to successive generations, it becomes a "marker", a genetic signpost. These signposts enable geneticists to follow the various branches of the human family tree back through time to their roots.

This is where it gets exciting. Thanks to The Genographic Project (2005-2007) of National Geographic, we now know that all of the branches of the human race from every continent can be traced to lineages that came out of Africa between 60,000 to 80,000 years ago. Using the markers/signposts found in the Y chromosome of males, geneticists have found a coalescence point, a common male ancestor (that the media was quick to call "Adam") who lived in Africa c. 60,000 years ago. Using the markers/signposts found in the mitochondrial DNA of females, geneticists have also found a coalescence point for female ancestors who lived 100,000 to 150,000 years ago; the media dubbed her "Eve" even though she lived thousands of years earlier than her counterpart. This female is NOT the one mother from whom all humans descend, but rather the carrier of a mtDNA molecule common to all female Homo sapiens, past and present.

To read further on this fascinating subject, I recommend the website of the Smithsonian Museum of Natural History. This site summarizes all the fossil, archaeological, and genetic evidence that shows an African origin for our species, Homo sapiens.

If the scribes who wrote Genesis knew what we know today, I think they would have been stunned, and perhaps a little disillusioned, to learn that we Homo sapiens came out of Africa about 60,000 years ago, and that other, even earlier Hominidae had already made their way from Africa into the Middle East, Europe and Asia—namely, Neanderthals and Denisovans.

In 2009 and 2010 their DNA was extracted from skeletal remains and analyzed. From the subsequent analysis, it was clear to geneticists that they were earlier ancestors of Homo sapiens. You may be surprised to learn that even though the Neanderthals and Denisovans are now extinct, a small percentage of their DNA lives on in us! To check your ancestral roots you may order a DNA kit from such sites as **23andme** through the internet.

I think this knowledge would have raised some important questions for the scribes of Genesis. What role did God have as Neanderthals, Denisovans, and Homo sapiens made their long and challenging journey out of Africa? How and why did the Neanderthals and Denisovans become extinct? Did they have souls? Was there an afterlife for the Neanderthals, Denisovans, and Homo sapiens who lived eons before the nomadic patriarchs of Mesopotamia? These are also metaphysical questions for us to ponder.

ADDENDUM C

The Ark: History or Folklore?

CONSIDER THE SIZE OF THE ARK AND THE NUMBER OF OCCUPANTS.

IT WAS 300 cubits long, 50 cubits wide and 30 cubits high. A cubit is the distance from the elbow to the fingertips. If a cubit is about 20 inches long, then the ark was 500 feet long, 83 feet wide and 50 feet high with three decks. In this space Noah had to accommodate all the animals, birds and reptiles of the world—thousands and thousands of species. How did Noah and his family catch and cage the animals, birds and insects? How did they locate animals indigenous only to Australia and the Galapagos Islands? Did they include predators such as tigers and lions, or Jurassic animals such as Tyrannosaurus Rex?

CONSIDER THE CONSTRUCTION OF THE ARK.

Noah and his family built the ark thousands of years prior to the Bronze Age before there were metal axes, saws or nails. They had to make the ark waterproof using pitch on the inside and outside. The building and waterproofing of the ark would have been a formidable, time-consuming task for a marine engineer with a crew of one hundred carpenters. Noah's family consisted of eight persons.

CONSIDER THE CARGO OF THE ARK.

Noah would have needed a great deal of storage space for food and fresh water—enough to last the forty days it rained, and the subsequent 150 days they lived in the ark. Many animals and birds require specific foods. Pandas, for example, eat twenty pounds of bamboo shoots daily. Imagine eight people looking after this humongous cargo. Think of the noise, the lack of light, the lack of ventilation and the smells.

The waters prevailed so mightily on the earth that all the high mountain under the whole heaven were covered . . . and all flesh died that moved upon the earth . . . and the waters prevailed on the earth for 150 days. (Genesis 7:19, 21)

CONSIDER THE AMOUNT OF WATER NEEDED TO SUBMERGE THE HIGH MOUNTAINS.

Our planet has more than one hundred mountains over 20,000 feet in height. Where did the water come from to cover these mountains? Even if all the glaciers melted during the forty days of rain, there still would not have been enough water to cover all the mountains. Some Christian apologists argue that the water came from the atmosphere. This argument fails to take into account the thermodynamic principle of condensation—when a vapor turns into water, heat is generated. Vast quantities of water would have been required. If this water came from atmospheric condensation, the heat that would have been released would have created a boiling sea of water in which nothing could survive.

LASTLY, CONSIDER THE CONSEQUENCES OF WATER COVERING THE EARTH.

After it had rained for forty days, it took 150 days for the water to recede and dry land to appear. Such an inundation would have killed all the trees and most plants. There would have been no "freshly plucked olive leaf" for a dove to find when set free from the ark (Genesis 8:11). There would have been no food for the plant-eating animals and birds and insects when they were released.

Commentary

It is highly likely that there was a disastrous flood that once inundated huge tracts of land between the Euphrates and Tigris Rivers. Stories of this flood would have been told in the succeeding generations. People must have speculated as to why such a tragedy had happened. The scribes had an explanation—due to rampant wickedness, God sent a flood that annihilated all life, except for one family.

Although we may not like this explanation, because it portrays God as a vengeful, heartless deity, we can appreciate the intent of the story. The scribes, with scant knowledge of ship construction, geology, biology, or climatology, were nonetheless religious leaders, and as such gave a theological explanation for the catastrophic flood that had once covered their "world".

Code of Ur-Nammu

(c. 2112-2095 BCE)

⁓⁓⁓⁓⁓⁓⁓

TWO FRAGMENTS OF a tablet inscribed with Sumerian laws were found at Nippur (in modern Nuffar, Iraq). They were transcribed by Samuel Kramer in 1952. (See *History begins at Sumer* by Samuel Kramer, University of Pennsylvania Press.)

FOLLOWING ARE 27 OF THE 30 RECONSTRUCTED LAWS:

1. If a man commits a murder, that man must be killed.
2. If a man commits a robbery, he will be killed.
3. If a man commits a kidnapping, he is to be imprisoned and pay fifteen shekels of silver.
4. If a slave marries a slave, and that slave is set free, he does not leave the household.
5. If a slave marries a free person, he/she is to hand the firstborn son over to his owner.
6. If a man violates the right of another and deflowers the virgin wife of a young man, they shall kill that male.
7. If the wife of a man followed after another man and he slept with her, they shall slay that woman, but that male shall be set free.

8. If a man proceeded by force, and deflowered the virgin female slave of another man, that man must pay five shekels of silver.

9. If a man divorces his first-time wife, he shall pay (her) one mina of silver.

10. If it is a (former) widow whom he divorces, he shall pay (her) half a mina of silver.

11. If the man had slept with the widow without there having been any marriage contract, he need not pay any silver.

12. If a man is accused of sorcery he must undergo ordeal by water; if he is proven innocent, his accuser must pay three shekels.

13. If a man accused the wife of a man of adultery, and the river ordeal proved her innocent, then the man who had accused her must pay one-third of a mina of silver.

14. If a prospective son-in-law enters the house of his prospective father-in-law, but his father-in-law later gives his daughter to another man, the father-in-law shall return to the rejected son-in-law two-fold the amount of bridal presents he had brought.

15. If a slave escapes from the city limits, and someone returns him, the owner shall pay two shekels to the one who returned him.

16. If a man knocks out the eye of another man, he shall weigh out one-half a mina of silver.

17. If a man has cut off another man's foot, he is to pay ten shekels.

18. If a man, in the course of a scuffle, smashed the limb of another man with a club, he shall pay one mina of silver.

19. If someone severed the nose of another man with a copper knife, he must pay two-thirds of a mina of silver.

20. If a man knocks out a tooth of another man, he shall pay two shekels of silver.

21. [*text destroyed...*] If he does not have a slave, he is to pay ten shekels of silver. If he does not have silver, he is to give another thing that belongs to him.

22. If a man's slave-woman, comparing herself to her mistress, speaks insolently to her, her mouth shall be scoured with one quart of salt.

Code of Ur-Nammu

23. If a slave woman strikes someone acting with the authority of her mistress, [*text destroyed...*]

24. If a man appeared as a witness, and was shown to be a perjurer, he must pay fifteen shekels of silver.

25. If a man appears as a witness, but withdraws his oath, he must make payment, to the extent of the value in litigation of the case.

26. If a man stealthily cultivates the field of another man and he raises a complaint, this is, however, to be rejected, and this man will lose his expenses.

✍ Author's Notes

A mina coin of silver was equal to fifty shekels (a unit of weight equivalent to 180 grains of barley).

Both the Sumerians and Babylonians sometimes determined the innocence or guilt of an accused by the "ordeal by water". If the accused survived, it was through the intervention of a god. (This practice also surfaced during the Inquisition.).

ADDENDUM E

Archaeological Evidence

~~~~~~~~~~~~~~~~~~

I N RECENT DECADES many cuneiform tablets have been discovered in the countries of the Middle East. These ancient tablets (along with previously discovered obelisks, stelae, stone pillars and engraved slabs) provide a chronological and political framework for the Old Testament. For example, the Merneptah Stele and the Amarna Letters show that Egypt was a major power in Canaan during the period of its settlement and the subsequent period of the Judges. Some of the Babylonian stelae relate to the Monarchy Era and provide specific information about military campaigns into Syria-Palestine.

AMARNA LETTERS (C.1360-1330 BCE)

These records, written on clay tablets in Akkadian cuneiform, were discovered in 1887 CE in the ancient city of Akhetaten, known today as Tell el-Amarna, Egypt. They are important because they show numerous diplomatic letters of correspondence between officials in Egypt and Canaan. The Amarna letter ANET 487-88 is interesting because it shows Abdi-Heba, a local chieftain of Jerusalem in the mid-1330's BCE, begging the Pharaoh not to blame him for a rebellion and pleading for the Pharaoh to send troops to re-establish Egypt's ownership over the lands.

THIS EGYPTIAN STELE, discovered in the city of Thebes in 1896 A.D., has been dated back to the reign of Pharaoh Merneptah. The final three lines of the hieroglyphic text are as follows: "The Canaan has been plundered into every sort of woe: Ashkelon has been overcome; Gezer has been captured; Yano'am is made non-existent. Israel is laid waste and his seed is not. Hurru is become a widow because of Egypt." Most biblical scholars think this text is the earliest reference to Israel outside of the Bible.

BUBASTITE PORTAL RELIEF (KARNAK, EGYPT C. 925 BCE)

David's name appears in a relief belonging to Pharaoh Soshenq I, who reigned from 943 to 922 BCE. This relief records the Pharaoh's conquests and military victories in Canaan. One of the carvings mentions the "Heights of David" in Southern Judah. The ruins of Karnak (including a once magnificent temple) are located between the ancient cities of Luxor and Thebes.

TEL DAN STELE (C. 870 TO 750 BCE)

Discovered in 1993/94 in northern Israel, the text on this broken stele (written in old Aramaic with a Phoenician alphabet) boasts of the victories of king Hazael of Damascus (reigned 843-806 BCE) over his enemies—including Omri, the king of Israel, and the "House of David". This claim is supported by a reference in 2 Kings 13:3, that Hazael conquered all of Israel.

THE MONOLITH INSCRIPTURE OF KING SHALMANESER III (R. 859-824 BCE)

This stele, discovered in 1861 in a Turkish town called Kurkh, records the first military campaign of Shalmaneser into Syria-Palestine. It describes the battle of Qarqar (853 BCE) in which Shalmaneser battled a coalition of twelve kings. One of the defending kings was "Ahab the Israelite" who contributed two thousand chariots and twenty thousand foot soldiers to the forces of the coalition.

Although the text describes the outcome as a great victory for the Assyrians, it was probably a stalemate because after the battle, Shalmaneser returned home.

BLACK OBELISK OF SHALMANESER III (C.858-824 BCE)

This impressive stone monument was discovered in 1846 in Northern Iraq and is displayed today in the British Museum in London. It commemorates Shalmaneser III receiving tribute from vassal kings including the Israelite King Jehu of the House of Omri (a reference to the kingdom of Israel). Jehu is shown bowing in obeisance on his hands and knees. As part of his humiliation, he is not wearing an outer garment.

MESHA STELE (C. 840 BCE)

This Moabite stele, discovered in 1868 at the site of ancient Dibon (now Dhiban, Jordan), tells a triumphant story of liberation as told by Mesha, the king of Moab. After many years of domination by the Israelites, Mesha fought against the Israelite king, Omri, and "triumphed over him and over his house and Israel has perished forever." The text describes in brutal detail how Mesha conquered the settlements of Ataroth, Nebo and Jahaz. Mesha gives credit to his god, Chemosh. The biblical account (2 Kings 3) has a different version of how this conflict ended. "And there came great wrath against Israel. And they withdrew from him and returned to their own land" (v.27). Israel did not perish. The Israelites strategically withdrew.

LACHISH RELIEF (C. 701 BCE)

Before Sennacherib attacked Jerusalem (c.701 BCE), he captured the fortified cities of Judah (Isaiah 36:1-2). One of the cities was Lachish (2

Chronicles 32:9) located 40 km southeast of Jerusalem. These events are recorded in a series of Assyrian palace bas-reliefs discovered in Nineveh in 1845-47. One of the inscriptions reads as follows: "Sennacherib, the mighty king, king of the country of Assyria, sitting on the throne of judgment, before the city of Lachish. I give permission for its slaughter." The artist who carved the pictures did not depict the siege of Jerusalem, presumably because the Assyrian forces were unsuccessful

SILOAM OR SHILOAH INSCRIPTURE (C.700 BCE)

King Hezekiah, fearing that the Assyrians would lay siege to Jerusalem, had a tunnel built to bring water into the city from a nearby spring (See 2 Kings 20:20). The tunnel was discovered in 1838, but it wasn't until 1880 that someone discovered an inscription inside the tunnel. Written in ancient Hebrew, the inscription records the construction of the tunnel. It has been dated to the 8th century BCE which parallels the reign of King Hezekiah and the unsuccessful siege of Jerusalem by the Assyrians led by Sennacherib.

On view in the British Museum in London, this barrel-shaped cylinder of baked clay was discovered in 1879 in the ruins of Babylon. The inscription (an Akkadian cuneiform script) denigrates Nabonidus, the Babylonian king who was deposed by Cyrus the Great. It details Cyrus' genealogy and royal titles depicting him as one chosen by the god Marduk to conquer and reign. He is praised for repairing ruined temples in the cities he conquered, restoring their cults and allowing captives to return to their homelands.

There is no mention of the battle of Opis and the subsequent slaughter of the army of Nabonidus. Nor is there any mention of Jews or Jerusalem. According to the Book of Ezra (1:1-4), Cyrus made a declaration, and also put it in writing, that the Lord had ordered him to build a temple in Jerusalem. Historians and archaeologists have not yet discovered this particular declaration.

BIBLIOGRAPHY

J. Maxwell Miller and John H. Hayes. *A History of Ancient Israel and Judah*. Philadelphia: The Westminster Press, 1986.

Finkelstein and Neil A. Silberman. *The Bible Unearthed*. New York: Touchstone Publishers, 2001.

D.M. Murdock. *Did Moses Exist? The Myth of the Israelite Lawgiver*. Seattle: Stellar House Publishing, 2014.

Joel M. Hoffman. *The Bible Doesn't Say That*. New York: St. Martin's Press, 2016.

E. A. Wallis Budge. *Book of the Dead*. New York: Dover Publications, 1967.

Anne Frank. *The Diary of a Young Girl*. New York, Doubleday Publishers, 1995.

John Gribbin. *A Brief History of Science*. Prospero Books, 2004.

INTERNET RESOURCES

Wikipedia – the free encyclopedia

The Jewish Encyclopedia

The Jewish Virtual Library

Encyclopedia Britannica

Schmoop: an educational website with summaries and analyses of biblical texts by PhD students from Stanford, Harvard and Berkeley.

MAKING SENSE OF THE OLD TESTAMENT
By Ronald V. Evans

The author welcomes any comments you wish to share on the contents of the book. If you found his book on the Old Testament informative and helpful, you may wish to read his book on the New Testament.

FAITH OF OUR FATHERS
Under the Microscope of Reason and History (2013)

In this book the author shares his research on such topics as the life of Jesus, authenticity of scripture, manuscript discrepancies, church schisms, the Crusades, and Intelligent Design or Evolution.

Some have found this book vindicating and liberating, while others have found it unsettling that a former minister with a M.Div. degree would question basic Christian tenets. This is a book that will challenge the reader to examine and evaluate his or her own faith. A hard copy may be purchased for $20 (Cnd.) plus $5 for s/h anywhere in North America. Please email the author to order a copy.

ronevans@sourcecable.net

Printed in Canada